"Deep, Sussman, and Stiber have created a poignant story that captures the true essence of leadership. You might think these lessons were obvious, but when you see the number of high profile leadership failures in the news today, you realize that leaders with these skills are sadly rare." —*Michael Mangan, Ph.D., strategy and change consultant, IBM Global Services*

"I thought I'd just start it, and found that I couldn't put it down. Once you get to the point where Larry is following Macon for the fishing "vacation," you really are hard pressed to stop the reading. Enjoyable! It is a very sound message for leadership in all walks of life." —*Lauren Patch, CEO, WYNCOM, Inc.*

"If you are looking for a book that will take you and your managers to the next level of leadership effectiveness, this text is a "must read." Combine this with an enjoyable read, and you have a great buy in your hands." —*Thomas S. Rittenhouse, president & CEO, Uniform Code Council, Inc.*

"I read *Lost and Found* from front to back without putting it down once, something I do only with Tom Clancy's books. This is a great book for all executives who are interested in improving their leadership and management styles, as did Larry. It is easy to read, understand, and certainly points you in the right direction. Good job!" —*Gideon Toeplitz, executive vice president and managing director, Pittsburgh Symphony*

"The meaning of leadership as it's understood by any leader will make or break that person as a leader. How deeply a leader can turn his staff into virtual partners who eagerly share his vision and help him realize his goals will ensure the success of all their efforts. Deep, Sussman, and Stiber's *Lost and Found* takes essential management credos and illustrates how one leader moves from an initial acceptance of those credos as mere management chestnuts to a realization that they are brief expressions of wisdom that really apply person to person in daily affairs. Digest this book and achieve results." —*Allan McGuffey, vice president and general manager, Emazing Services, a Sony subsidiary*

"A compelling story for all leaders who have faced the realities of their leadership styles in the workplace and personal lives!" —*Bill Kline, VP/chief learning officer, Delta Airlines*

"When the hero of *Lost and Found* learns that you can't win if other people lose, he learns the essential truth of leadership. And how he learns it makes for some great reading." —*William J. Zalewski, senior vice president–investments, UBS PaineWebber*

"In a world driven by speed, efficiency, and performance, we often lose sight of the importance of process. We become so entrenched in conquering the current landscape that we significantly undervalue how our actions impact others. The authors of this book present a story of one man's journey in gaining new personal insights after being forced to reflect upon his own leadership deficiencies. Such a story becomes a real gift to those of us muddling through our own circumstances. Perhaps it could even prevent us from wandering off our own personal cliffs through the application of some simple leadership principles." —*Michael J. Arena, Ph.D., director of organizational effectiveness, Ingersoll-Rand*

"I am in a business where I need to keep up with the business publications of the day. Most I read dutifully; this one captured me and grabbed my attention as few others have. Every one of our employees is encouraged to read *Lost and Found*. I want each of them to learn the life lessons embedded in Know, Grow, and Own for themselves and for the people they lead. As for me, I plan to reread the book every time I find myself assuming I'm doing the right thing to grow my people and be the most empowering leader I can be." —*Nancy Lauterbach, CEO, Five Star Speakers & Trainers*

"A great book that I could not put down. This was fun to read while prompting insight. I found myself in the book, as well as my colleagues. Know, Grow and Own will be a new credo for me." —*Allen S. Thomas, Jr., national managing partner for Partner Matters, Deloitte & Touche*

LOST & FOUND

OTHER BOOKS BY THE AUTHORS

LOST & FOUND

THE STORY OF HOW ONE MAN DISCOVERED
THE SECRETS OF LEADERSHIP . . .
WHERE HE WASN'T EVEN LOOKING

Lyle Sussman, PH.D.,

Sam Deep, *and*

Alex Stiber

CROWN
BUSINESS
NEW YORK

This is a work of fiction. All incidents and dialogue, and all
the characters, are products of the authors' imagination,
but the lessons are real.

Published by Crown Business, New York, New York.
Member of the Crown Publishing Group, a division of
Random House, Inc.
www.randomhouse.com

CROWN BUSINESS and colophon are trademarks of
Random House, Inc.

Printed in the United States of America

Design by Robert C. Olsson

Library of Congress Cataloging-in-Publication Data
Sussman, Lyle, 1944–
Lost & Found : the story of how one man discovered the
secrets of leadership . . . where he wasn't even looking /
Lyle Sussman, Sam Deep, and Alex Stiber.
p. cm.
1. Leadership. 2. Delegation of powers. 3. Time management.
I. Deep, Samuel D. II. Stiber, Alex, 1950– III. Title.
HD57.7.S87 2004
658.4'092—dc21 2003007649
ISBN 1-4000-5085-5 (Hardcover)

10 9 8 7 6 5 4 3 2 1

First Edition

CONTENTS

LOST & FOUND

PART ONE

CHAPTER ONE

Why Me?

"Welcome back from the leadership workshop, Larry."

Startled, Larry Parks bolted up from his painstaking inspection of the blueprints for KGO Worldwide Conveyance Company's major project in Singapore. The plans involved an intricate web of moving ground-level and elevated walkways, escalators, and elevators throughout a stretch of central Singapore. Larry's boss in the Excalibur Engineering division, Chloe Hall, was leaning in his doorway. He set down his mechanical pencil and mustered a half-smile.

"Hey, Chloe. What's up?"

"Just wanted to know how the workshop went."

"Great," Larry said, trying to feign enthusiasm. "*Really* good."

"Can you stop by my office in about fifteen minutes to talk about it?"

Chloe was turning to leave as Larry managed, "Sure." To himself he thought, *It's 7:15 Monday morning. Can't she at least let me deal with my e-mail before demanding an audience?*

Larry rubbed his closed eyes with the cool fingers of both hands. He leaned forward, elbows on the gel wrist pad in front of his keyboard, and held his face in his hands while his inbox opened, revealing a torrent of e-mails awaiting his response:

"Need your help."

"Problems with permits."

"URGENT . . . supplier financial troubles."

"Timeline revision."

"Staffing shortfall."

"Technical glitch."

"Spec change. . . . "

Larry had tried to keep on top of e-mail during his absence. Even so, he counted two dozen new messages from Singapore having to do with *the project*—or, as he'd come to refer to it, "The road to hell." There were another ten from members of his domestic team.

Of the thirty-four total project-related messages, twelve were marked URGENT.

And all had arrived since he'd left the office the previous afternoon—Sunday, when people were supposed to be with their families.

Larry let his head hang down and massaged the back of his neck, tracing along the spine to soothe the tension building there. But when he looked back up at his computer screen, he felt his jaw tighten again. "Oh, *brother*," he muttered through clenched teeth. "How can there be this many new e-mails on a Monday morning? Doesn't anybody around here take a break? Can't anybody think for himself? Do I have to personally handle *every single detail*?"

Larry turned toward the wall behind him and caught his reflection in a large framed photograph of his father straining to reel in a huge marlin on a charter boat in the Bahamas. He considered all the time he'd wasted attending that leadership-development workshop the previous week, and the additional pressure it had put on him. The circles darkening under his eyes reminded him of how badly he wanted one really good night's sleep.

Larry put aside the project plan and pulled out his workshop notes to prepare for his meeting with Chloe.

Looking at the sparse pages from the workshop, Larry recalled the trouble he'd had paying attention. He knew its focus was developing leadership skills and self-awareness. But he'd had other things on his mind.

Larry had brought the project plan to the workshop, plus the work breakdowns, Gantt charts, resource-allocation tables, and a bunch of component drawings he needed to review as well. He'd hoped to find a seat in the back of the room where he could be left alone to do his work while "getting his dance card punched." But the tables and chairs in the room were arranged in a horse-shoe that had left Larry no place to hide.

He'd resigned himself, about halfway through the first of the three days, to being an active participant in the workshop. But he still found it hard to care. The training was all soft: talk about the importance of process, caring for your people, and other principles that Larry thought were just so much window dressing.

What had Chloe said? Oh, yes: "When you started working here, I saw a potential leader for this company, not just a brilliant engineer or a competent project manager. This is a tough culture, with lots of *guys* who have a storm-the-castle-worry-about-casualties-later attitude. And the people, like you, who bring the highest level of technical expertise don't always bring an equivalent level of people skills. But from watching you work with others, I think you have the *potential* to turn into a real leader. You've always shown yourself to accept feedback and to be open to change. I want to get you off to the best possible start on this assignment, and this workshop has produced strong results for lots of people."

Larry had looked forward to hearing what his mentor, Macon, would make of all this, and wondered why Macon hadn't had to attend as well—then remembered Macon had already been to it, or something like it, last year.

When talk in the workshop had turned to the importance of delegating thoughtfully, Larry recalled Macon's advice: "If you want to make sure something's done right, you either do it yourself or double-check to make sure the guy you assigned it to didn't screw it up." That was more practical advice, Larry thought, and it didn't take three whole days to deliver.

A lot of good going off to a workshop did me, Larry thought on his way to Chloe's corner office. *The real work-*

shop is here, where there's work to be done, and she sent me off to a hotel for three days to play leadership games.

"Larry," Chloe acknowledged as he entered, looking up from some papers on her large, dark, orderly, polished wooden desk.

Must be some rare imported rosewood, Larry guessed. He couldn't help but compare it to his own desk, made of some sort of vinyl laminate that failed to even remotely resemble the granite its pattern was designed to simulate.

"Have a seat. And tell me, how did it go at Jim Enos's workshop?" Chloe showed him her confident smile.

Larry took a deep breath and recollected his experience of the previous week.

CHAPTER TWO

The Masquerade

"Good stuff," Larry said, trying to sound convincing. "I'm not sure I agree with Enos's take on everything, but there were some good principles I think I can apply. It, uh, reinforced some of the things I don't think I was paying enough attention to."

Chloe walked around her desk to take a seat next to Larry. He reflected that in her spacious, sunlit office, with its French Impressionist prints, off-white walls, light gray carpeting, and bright but soft light, he ought to feel more relaxed. Instead, he often felt on edge, intimidated. Maybe it was Chloe's strong, angular chin that threw him off balance, he reflected.

Though he was glad to be out of the harsh fluorescent light of his own office and in a room with a view of woods, he was nonetheless put off slightly by the obvious disparity in his and Chloe's organizational status. And he caught himself wondering how, given their proximity in age

(Chloe was only three years older) and his superior training as an engineer, she had advanced so much further
than he had. *On paper,* he thought, *you'd figure she'd be reporting to me.*

"Like what, Larry?" Chloe asked.

"Do you mind if I look at my notes? There was so much
that it hasn't all sunk in yet," Larry offered.

"Of course, go ahead. I hadn't meant it to be this for-
mal, but I'm interested in your observations."

Larry opened his organizer and scanned what he'd
written under *Day One*:

> A leader's job is to create and manage the cul-
> ture??? (While I'm doing this, who's minding the store?)
>
> You're only as good as the people who work for
> you. (Need better people on my team.)
>
> Leading is freeing people to do what they need to
> do. (I'd like to free a couple of people on my team to
> go find another job!)
>
> Managers can't lead without awareness of their im-
> pact on others. (How do I find out if I'm getting through
> to them?)
>
> If you expect to sit in the shade, you'll need to
> plant trees. (Is this a gardening seminar? When you
> need a meal *now*, you don't seed a vegetable garden.)

That sure wasn't what Chloe wanted to hear. Flipping
the page, and hoping for help, Larry checked what he'd
written under the title *Action Items from Workshop*:

1. Leave voice mail reminding everyone on team to focus more closely on their piece of the action and the bottom line. *Let them know I mean business.*

2. Send e-mail to team members telling them to list the things that have gone awry because of lack of skill or knowledge and then send it to me. Use list to get some technical backup.

3. Check with Chloe to see whether there's any way to change project bonus structure to reward people with stock instead of straight pay. That oughtta focus people more on making sure that their work contributes to the bottom line.

Larry decided it would be better to generalize. He leaned back in his chair and placed his hands, tent-style, in front of him, a gesture he'd learned conveyed confidence. "Well, I came away with basic things about paying more attention to what my people are doing, making sure they know how to do their jobs, promoting responsibility," Larry offered.

"Good points, Larry. Okay, you pass the general content quiz."

Larry absorbed Chloe's sarcasm, wondering what it meant.

"And what I hear you saying is that none of this is especially new to you?" she probed, tilting her head slightly.

"Well, you know, not really *new*, but maybe things that in the daily shuffle get lost. I realize I need to lift my sights a little higher but still keep my eye on the ball."

Chloe's lips tightened, then relaxed. For a second Larry

thought she was going to say something critical, but she seemed to accept what he said—even if she wasn't happy about it. "Okay, Larry," Chloe said. "I just wanted to welcome you back, to tell you how much we're all counting on you for a big win here. You can come to me for anything you need. My door's always open."

"Thanks, boss," Larry said as he stood up to leave. Chloe gave him a tight smile, and he mischievously pulled the door closed behind him.

Walking back to his office wide-eyed, Larry felt that he had just narrowly dodged a bullet. He decided to call Macon to get his advice on how to handle this business with the workshop and Chloe. After all, Macon had been through it before and survived.

CHAPTER THREE

Now What?

When Larry got back to his office, his phone was lit up—message light blinking, new call ringing. He picked up the receiver.

"Larry, it's Miles. We've got a contract problem with the cable supplier. They've decided now that they won't knock off the five percent we thought they'd agreed to. And we can't find anything in writing that says they ever agreed to that."

"Damn it, Miles, I can't believe you didn't get it *in writing*! How'd this happen? You've been a purchasing manager for—how long is it?"

"Look, Larry, *how* it happened doesn't get us to a solution. And my competence as a purchasing manager is between me and my boss, not you. You can't just throw this ball in my court and then turn your back and walk away. You're the project manager here, not me. If you want to go around looking for who to blame instead of working with me on a solution to this, then look in the mirror. So what do you want to do about it?"

"Okay, Miles, calm down. Let's round up the usual suspects and have a quick meeting on this. See you in ten minutes in the war room."

It sounded to Larry as if Miles might have cracked the handset when he hung up the phone.

Before Larry could get up to leave his office, however, the phone rang again. The caller ID screen said it was his lead designer, John Burke.

Against his better judgment, Larry picked up the phone. "Listen, John, I'm on my way to a meeting. What's up?"

"Here it is in a nutshell, Larry. You've looked over the drawings pretty carefully, right?"

"Well, I tried. But Chloe had me in this training thing for a couple of days, as I think you know, and I haven't had the time to look at them as closely as I wanted."

"Then you probably wouldn't have noticed this, but whoever did them needs to go back to basic training. They stamped just about everything 'critical to quality.' It's like they never heard about how to incorporate customer requirements in determining CTQs. If we have to QC everything they marked, this project'll go way over budget, and way behind schedule."

Larry sat down and massaged his temples with his free hand. "John, why the heck are you making this *my* problem? Can't you just go back to the design engineer and ask him to revise them?"

"Not if he hasn't been to the Quality Function Deployment course, I can't. He won't know why I'm bothered by this. And if he *has* been through QFD, then he flunked. This is not a job for entry-level engineers, Larry. We need the most experienced, brightest, and hardest-working people on this project. The risks are just too high."

"They always are," Larry sighed, trying to end the conversation. "All right, John, I'll get right on it."

John continued: "When you picked this guy, didn't you look to see whether he'd been through QFD?"

"What makes you think *I* picked him?"

"Hey, you're the manager, Larry. Isn't it your call who's on the team? And even if you didn't pick him, didn't you check to *see* if he'd been to QFD? And if not, why didn't you send him?"

"John, I don't need to explain myself to you. And this isn't getting us anywhere. I'll check the drawings myself," Larry said.

"Oh, and by the way, Larry, it may be beside the point by now, but don't you think it would be worthwhile to get the marketing manager and sales engineer in the room with the core team as soon as possible so that guys like this novice engineer can get the big picture straight from the photographer's lens?"

"Why's that, John?"

"Because, Larry, those are the guys who had the initial customer contact, the primary vision for the project, and they're the best ones to represent what the customer expects—what they have *bought*. I shouldn't have to tell you how things can get distorted once they move into the hands of engineers and designers."

Larry sighed again, remembering the lessons from previous training about the importance of keeping core teams intact through a project's life cycle. "I'll see what I can do, John."

"You know, sometimes I feel like you've given us a thousand-piece puzzle and asked us to complete it without ever seeing the picture on the box. Maybe it's not the design engineer's fault about these drawings."

"I said I'll look into it, John," Larry said, and hung up. *What next?* he thought. *Oh yeah—Miles's meeting.*

By the end of the day, Larry had become aware of two more important problems. There were bugs in programmable-controller logic that he'd been assured had been fixed. And a key member of the implementation sub-team, Dave, reported that his father had died and he was taking the rest of the week off for bereavement leave.

Of course, Larry knew the value of bereavement leave. But he questioned Dave's commitment to the project, in light of the voice-mail greeting he left: "I'll be out of the office for several days, and won't be monitoring voice mail or e-mail." *I know how hard this must be on you, Dave,* Larry thought, *but you can't find a few minutes to check e-mail at the end of each day?*

CHAPTER FOUR

Safe at Home?

Driving home at 7:30, Larry felt that he hadn't made much progress during the day. The project's problems had taken on a life of their own during his short absence at the leadership-training seminar. But he assured himself that he could regain control with a firm, hands-on approach. Maybe a few heads had to roll to set things straight.

Larry remembered now that he'd intended to ask Macon for advice. His old supervisor always had a way of putting things in their proper perspective, Larry thought. He made a mental note to call Macon after supper.

First, though, he was looking forward to the chance to talk with his wife, Jessie, about the mounting problems at work. He knew he could count on her for insight and an understanding ear.

But when Larry got home, he found the table cleared, the lights off in the kitchen, and no sign of anyone downstairs.

At the beginning of the Singapore project, he'd told

Jessie and their kids that he'd have to put in late hours at the office. This certainly wasn't the first time in his career that he'd needed to sacrifice family time. So even if he hadn't called this evening to say he'd be late, Larry couldn't understand why Jessie hadn't left a plate out for him or, better still, waited to eat with him.

When he found her upstairs, cleaning her closet, he tried to strike up a conversation by running down the events of the day: "It started with John Burke calling me—no, it started before that, with Miles . . . "

After a while, Jessie put down a dress and looked at Larry, her lips pursed while she considered what to say. Finally, she coolly observed, "You know, Larry, it sounds as though you think you have to solve all the problems yourself."

"That's just it, Jess. I do. I'm the boss. All day long, everyone's coming to me, telling me what's wrong and asking me either what *I'm* going to do about it or what *I* think *they* should do about it. We've got a lot of bright people around there. I don't understand why they won't think for themselves and come to me with solutions rather than a parade of problems." Larry felt his frustration level rising.

Jessie went back to arranging and folding her clothes. "Is there anything that you've done that might lead them to act that way?" she asked. "Maybe you *let* them all dump on you. Or it's possible that you take over so often that they don't feel like they *can* do it on their own. You know, sometimes I see you doing that with the kids."

Larry felt slightly hurt. "Why do you say that?"

"Because it's true, honey. I know it's a tough line to walk, especially for someone with perfectionist leanings. You feel that since the work's got to be up to your high standards, you have to stand over people while they do it. And when you do that, you make people nervous; they mess up, so you take over."

"But that's just it. I *do* have high standards. And this project *is* critical. And if it doesn't go according to plan, it's *my* butt, since I'm the manager."

"I know, Larry," Jessie said, giving him a sympathetic half-smile. "You have to admit, though, that there's an element of the self-fulfilling prophecy in what's going on."

"You're saying I *want* it to fail?"

"Not at all. I'm saying you expect other people to do less than their best and fail to meet your standards. And then maybe you create the conditions so that that's just what happens."

"Well, I'm under a lot of pressure, and I can't afford any more missteps on my team. I thought you'd be more understanding about it."

Jessie sighed. "I'm trying to help you, Larry. And it's not easy because, well, you have to admit that under pressure you tend to make a lot of excuses. And sometimes it just gets a little hard, you know?"

She walked over to the bed and sat down, smoothing a spot and patting it for Larry to sit next to her. She tilted her head until he did so, then continued.

"You work twelve-hour days, weekends, then take off for a workshop, come back and go to work on a Sunday, then you come home, and pretty much all you talk about is work. This kind of life sure isn't what *I* bargained for. Is it *really* what you want?"

Larry felt his heart sink in his chest. Leading a project this large at last wasn't supposed to be like this. It was a big opportunity, a major step in a career he'd been building for fourteen years, and not only was it going poorly at work, but now here was Jessie telling him that the tension was eating into their home life.

Answering her question, he said, "I *thought* so. I thought this was what *we* wanted."

Jessie's voice rose somewhat with her incredulity. "*We* wanted you to be working seventy or more hours a week, then coming home like a tired old tugboat, towing your barge of misery behind you? How could that be what *we* wanted?"

"Ah, come on, Jessie," Larry said, his voice hurt but tired. "Today was unbelievable. And the icing on the cake is what Chloe messaged me at the end of the day: She's arranged for that trainer, Jim Enos, to come and talk to me about building my team. Because apparently people are complaining about my leadership skills."

"Well, listen, Larry," Jessie said, softening a little. "Maybe that will help. Anyway, enough of this for now. Why don't we go downstairs and get you something to eat?"

While Larry wolfed down a cheese omelet and a salad, Jessie ran down the domestic news. During dessert their kids, David and Jennifer, dropped into the kitchen to say a perfunctory hello and grab snacks to get them through the rest of their homework.

When Larry had finished eating, it was almost nine o'clock. He decided he'd wait until morning to call Macon.

CHAPTER FIVE

Macon the Lionhearted

"Lawrence of Excalibur," Macon bellowed into the phone when Larry called him the next morning at work. "How's my proudest accomplishment? Still strutting around like a peacock after beating me out for project lead on the Singapore installation? Word around here has it that you're on an escalator to the stars!"

"I hope you're not—"

"Don't worry about it, Larry," Macon interrupted. "You're heading up, and I'm on the elevator that keeps getting stuck between floors. That's the way it goes, I guess. Hey, until someone comes in to replace Chloe, my fortunes aren't gonna change."

"I hear you." Larry tried to sound empathetic, though he wasn't sure Macon would notice. "Say, you got some time to meet with me this morning? There's some things I want to talk over with you about the project."

"Sure, get us a conference room and some coffee, and I'll see you in half an hour, if that works for you."

"I'll let you know where," Larry said.

Larry hadn't sat down with his mentor for a few months. First Macon had gone off to a leadership workshop, and then he suddenly flew to Europe to—in his own words—"rescue a failing project there." He'd stayed over to lead project-management workshops at Global Headquarters, and finally took his first vacation in years.

When Larry had been hired at Excalibur, Macon had been the one interviewer with whom Larry had been particularly impressed, given Macon's obviously superior technical knowledge and what Larry had seen as a take-no-prisoners attitude. Shortly after starting there, Larry had approached Macon and proposed the mentor relationship, and Macon had gladly accepted, joking in a pompous, ceremonial tone, "When I've conquered the world, my boy, I will pass the sword to you. I am confident that under my tutelage, you will have become ready to accept the magic and the awesome responsibility forged in its metal."

Entering the conference room now, Larry saw that Macon was already there, looking out the window.

"Whattaya see out there?" Larry asked.

Macon laughed. "Bunch o' turkeys strutting across the parking lot."

"Hey, be careful what you say about the leadership team," Larry joked, closing the door.

Macon snorted. "No, really. There's a bunch of wild turkeys in the parking lot. Musta come out of the woods back there. So, anyway, what was it you need to talk about?"

As Macon turned toward him, Larry noticed that his short, gray hair was a little tousled, and the pouches under his eyes were even darker than usual. Apparently the vacation hadn't been the rest he needed, or the guy was just too tired to recover any remnant of his old energy.

Larry thought about what to discuss first. "Well, I'm mainly thinking about this leadership workshop Chloe sent me to last week. I think it's the same one she sent you to. Led by a guy named Enos."

"Then watch out, my boy, 'cause ever since then it's been nothing but the down escalator for me."

"Funny, I thought that when they send you to these things it means they're grooming you."

"You'd think so. But I'm guessing in my case it's more like sending a car into the shop for an overhaul, trying to get a few more miles out of it before you replace it with a spiffy new model."

"I can't believe that, Macon. You've got more technical knowledge than the rest of these folks combined."

"Yeah, but see how much that counts for these days," Macon protested, taking a sip of the coffee Larry had put on the table. "All they talk about now is–," Macon paused for dramatic effect, grimaced, and raised his hands to make little quotation marks in the air, "Caring for People. Leadership. Empowerment. Vision. Teamwork."

Coming out of Macon's mouth, those words sounded almost like expletives. Larry had to stifle a laugh. The guy would never change.

"Anyway," Larry said after a pause to sip his own coffee, "I wanted to talk about how you handled Chloe after you came back from the workshop. I get the feeling she's looking for something, and I don't think I'm showing it to her."

"You're right on there, my boy. Because you know, and I bear you no resentment for this, my name was up there for manager of the Singapore project. It was *mine*, buddy, and that's why they sent me to that workshop. Then, only two days after I got back, they changed their plans and told me that project in Europe was in technical trouble and no one else could clean it up, and so blah blah blah, here we are."

"I never knew that," Larry said, shaking his head and grimacing. "Although I *was* surprised they gave it to me instead of you."

"Ah, disappointed you weren't their first choice?" Macon asked. "Don't be. They got the right guy. But lemme give you some tips on what *not* to do if you don't want to follow in my lame footsteps."

"Shoot," Larry said, grateful that Macon was always willing to be generous with advice.

"First, and most important: Don't let on with Chloe that you think the leadership workshop was a crock. That was my mistake—being honest." He looked briefly off in the distance and shook his head, obviously recalling some strained meeting just after he'd returned. "Heck, any dummy knows that if she spends money sending you there, you gotta pretend it was worth it. I just couldn't help myself, I guess. Never been much good at 'managing up.' "

Larry remembered how hard he'd found it to feign

enthusiasm in his conversation with Chloe. "What did you tell her?" he asked.

"Everything she didn't want to hear, and nothing she did."

Larry couldn't help wondering at the defiant pride in Macon's voice.

"I told her I thought Enos was an arrogant SOB, selling snake oil, and that she'd have made a smarter use of her investment in my success by giving me the money to use as incentive pay to motivate my team."

"Well, that's a reasonable point," Larry said, appreciating Macon's practicality.

"Yeah, to you and to me. But not Chloe. She's got this ridiculous idea that money doesn't motivate people. In her view, it's all about leadership, whatever *that* means. But, hey, she asked me, and I tell it like I see it. You know me, maybe I'm not the most political. But I'm no one's fool; I don't pander to anyone. She asked me what I brought back from the workshop that I thought I could use going forward, and I showed her some engineering sketches I'd made. That ended our meeting. Next day, I get the news they need me in Europe."

"Damn. How'd you respond to that?"

"I told her I knew it was a demotion. I said, 'You know, I don't see anything in my performance plan that says I need to be soft on people.' "

"And then?"

"Get this. Chloe tells me, 'Macon, I've told you in so many words, again and again. Why do you think I sent you to those training seminars? Why do you think I got you the three-sixty-degree feedback?' I told her I thought she was doing that just to punish me," Macon finished, and forced a self-conscious laugh.

Larry managed half a grin. "What did Chloe say to that?"

"She said, 'Well, I guess I can't expect a leopard to change his spots.' And on *that* I agreed with her."

Larry took another sip of coffee and thought. "Speaking of wild cats," he joked, "I once heard one of those training guys say that if you could train a man-eating lion not to eat his handler, you could train anyone to do anything, nature or not."

"Maybe," Macon admitted tentatively, "But lions aren't people, you know what I mean? So let me give you some advice, Larry."

"What's that?"

"Fake it. Play along. You know all the words, all the things to say about empowering people, leveraging the synergy of diverse opinions, delegating responsibility. All that crap. Spout 'em like you're a fountain. Chloe eats that stuff up. Tell her what she wants to hear so you can keep her off your back, and then go do your job. Just make sure you don't let this stuff get in the way. Remember, Chloe's shooting for VP of Global Sales, and she gets everything she wants, so you won't have to deal with her forever. If you're lucky, the pendulum will swing back your way with her replacement, and you'll have someone who understands the power of the stick. Who knows? Maybe if you play the part convincingly enough, *you'll* have her job in a year or two."

CHAPTER SIX

Why Is This Happening?

At work the next morning (or was it the day after that? or three days later? all the days were starting to become a blur of activity), Larry found thirty-two new project-related e-mails waiting for him from Singapore, along with two voice-mail messages marked URGENT.

"Don't they sleep over there?" he said out loud to his empty office. Then he remembered the time difference and bemoaned the inconvenience of managing across the International Date Line.

But worse than the e-mails from Singapore were an almost equal number of messages from members of his own team—half e-mail, half voice-mail.

"Why don't these cowards just come and talk to me directly?" Larry complained out loud, again to no one. *Why do they play hit-and-run with our messaging systems? Why are they all stumbling around as if they're lost in the woods somewhere?*

It was when Larry considered the content of the messages, though, that the alarms really started to ring in his head. In sum, the messages seemed to be adding up to a warning:

Unless Larry Parks does something radical NOW, this project will miss its critical targets, and he'll be the one they hang.

A couple of days later, Larry found himself firing off a number of terse, occasionally caustic, e-mail and voice-mail responses, emphasizing the need for people on the project to stop wasting time and money *complaining* about what's not working and start focusing on how to meet their deadlines and budgets by *fixing* what's not working.

"Deadlines are NOT NEGOTIABLE on this project," he wrote in a message to the entire project team. "If you haven't found a way to meet them, you're spending your time looking in the wrong places. Stop telling me about problems and start bringing me solutions. FOCUS is what we need now. You're on this team because you have a reputation for knowing how to do your job. You've earned respect for your past accomplishments. But this is not the past. No one around here gets to rest on his laurels. So it's time to find a way to make this project work. We know what our budget is, and we know when this project is to be completed. I don't think I need to remind you that our CEO is equally aware of those targets! You all heard him speak at the last all-employees meeting: No one gets to take his job for granted."

Larry reread that message before sending it off. He liked its tone—*strong and direct,* he thought. *And motivational, too. Sometimes, all it takes to get people in gear is a good swift kick in the butt.*

He then called his assistant and asked her to cancel his dentist appointment. The annual checkup would have to wait. "I'll do that, Larry," she said. "And Fred Harken's waiting to see you."

Fred was the senior manufacturing engineer, a man after Larry's heart: a seasoned, gruff engineer from the old school. Fred didn't believe in "teams"; he believed in obedient staff who knew what their jobs were and did them without question.

He didn't believe in "team leaders"; he believed in functional managers who knew how to quantify people's contributions and make heads roll when they weren't pulling their weight.

He didn't believe in "team ownership of outcomes"; he believed in "doing your job and doing it right the first time so that no one else has to do it for you and you don't have to do it over again."

He especially didn't believe in "vision." He enunciated that word with sarcastic contempt: "*Vision* is for flakes. Show me the details." In short, as Fred was known to say, "If it don't say 'ouch' when you hit it, you're too soft and fuzzy."

And Fred believed that Larry needed to get control of this project.

"Listen, Larry, I know you're between a rock and a hard place here. You've got to make tight numbers with a lean staff. But that doesn't excuse you for not getting back to me on this problem." Fred jabbed his finger at a blueprint on Larry's conference table.

"Before throwing this over the wall to me, your lead designer didn't consult with me about how we were going to be able to *shape* the steel on this box." He circled a spot on the blueprint with a pencil. "John formed something that looks very nice on paper, very aesthetic. I'm sure he and his imagination had a great time together while he was drawing this fantasy. But I can't find a supplier for the equipment it will take to make this thing at anywhere near affordable cost. They'll have to invent, not adapt, and we said from the beginning that 'no inventing' was key to meeting our targets for speed, cost, and quality. If you'd brought me in at the beginning of the planning stage instead of waiting until I finally showed up on your project plan as accountable for action, we wouldn't be in this fix. From now on, I'm working directly with you on this, not through John."

Fred's stern message to Larry was the harbinger of a series of even more stressful interactions that would occur over the next two days. Department heads kept insisting they wanted to deal directly with Larry, not Larry's people. When Jessie called in the afternoon to ask, "Hi, sweet tooth, how did your dental appointment go?", Larry snapped at her:

"I don't have three hours right now to have my teeth cleaned!"

"Feeling stressed today?"

"Stressed?" he complained sarcastically. "Do I sound stressed? Go figure!" At the end of the conversation, Larry added, "Oh, by the way, Jess, don't hold up dinner for me. I've got a meeting here till nine, so I'll snack out of the vending machines."

The rest of that week reminded Larry of the nor'easter that had hit the previous February: He'd woken up at five A.M. to shovel his driveway clear of snow, and at six he had to do it all over again. Complaints just kept piling up, falling so unremittingly that he felt he was digging out all week.

The next week's blizzard hit the first thing Monday morning. One of the site managers in Singapore called with the news that a government safety inspector was holding up the release of permits based on flawed paperwork submitted as part of the application process. As a result, trucks with materials couldn't be unloaded at the site. The trucking company was planning to return all materials to their point of origin, charging for hauling, loading, and unloading both ways, and so on.

Larry had never been entirely comfortable with applying the just-in-time approach to manufacturing on a project of this nature and complexity, but he'd accepted it as a given, because the company had embraced it as its "flavor of the month," as Macon was wont to say of so many new initiatives mandated from the executive suite. It wasn't like building a car or a computer, where just-in-time concepts were employed in order to minimize costs tied up in inventory. This was a far more complex system of interdependent processes relying on people to stay on top not only of their own tasks but of how those tasks interacted with others, Larry thought, and a greater margin for error was required.

So now, the company's just-in-time philosophy had failed in this project because, Larry realized, he'd trusted someone to do a job and it hadn't gotten done. The human factor had been the weak link in the complex network.

Larry kicked himself, too, because the site coordinator had told him that they weren't getting enough information to complete the applications on time. He'd treated that as a minor matter, compared to everything else.

"Why is this happening?" Larry said out loud as he watched the snowdrifts pile higher.

On top of the performance blunders, staffing problems started to develop. Dave came back from bereavement leave, worked distractedly for a few weeks, then put in a request with Chloe for a six-month "sabbatical." It bothered Larry that Dave had gone straight to Chloe rather than to him, and it infuriated him that Chloe granted it without even asking for his input as Project Manager. But expressing his anger toward Chloe was, he knew, unwise, and anyway the practical need to scramble to backfill for Dave was more pressing. That meant bringing in a contractor who didn't know the project at all, needed time to get up to speed, and had only a dubious commitment to the project's long-term success.

But, Larry rationalized, *maybe using contractors is a better strategy in the long run. No one has any loyalty to the company anymore anyway. Everyone's just looking out for himself, planning his next career move. And if contractors don't work out, you don't need to fire them; you just don't give them any more work, and get someone else.*

Then Larry's assistant put in a request with HR for a transfer. He assured himself, *She can easily be replaced. There'll be five people fighting over her job. It's not like it's a high-skilled job.* But interviewing candidates meant he had yet another task that as far as he could see added no value to the project.

And so the weeks passed, the mini-crises came and went, chewing up time and resources. The e-mails and voice mails piled up, and the schedule slipped and slipped, as Larry tried to make a good show of keeping his confidence high while privately feeling it erode into misery and helplessness.

In the midst of a typically frustrating afternoon, Chloe's knock on the doorjamb interrupted Larry's reflections.

"Do you have time to come to my office now, Larry?" she asked. "I've got Jim Enos with me. He's got some insights from the recent culture survey and the three-sixty we'd like to discuss with you."

In his head Larry heard himself saying, *No, I do not have time for this culture crap. I have work to do on the most critical project at KGO, and these distractions about stuff that's not even remotely related are costing us all a lot of money.* But with only the trace of a sigh, he said, "Sure, let's hear what Jim's got to say."

CHAPTER SEVEN

The Wake-Up Call

Entering Chloe's sunlit office, Larry met Jim Enos's outstretched hand and returned a firm shake. Larry thought of leadership consultants as fast-talking salesmen, more or less, so he was always surprised at how ordinary Enos looked: not slick, average height, off-the-rack suit, hair receding at both temples. *If this guy cared about real numbers instead of goose grease,* Larry thought, *I'd be glad to have him on my team.*

"I hear you've got information that Chloe thinks can help me," Larry said, direct as always. He wanted to get straight to whatever the consultant had come to say so he could get beyond it and back to work.

"Yes, Larry," Jim confirmed. "But before we get into it, I want to share something with you relating to why I'm even here today."

"As I said, Chloe already told me," Larry said, defensively.

Jim cleared his throat and looked at Chloe, who nodded to him. "Here's the deal, Larry, and I'm giving it to you unvarnished. There are a lot of people around here demanding your head. The only reason I'm here talking to you today is that you've got an influential champion in Chloe. You're not the only one who's in the hot seat here. In standing up for you, Chloe's putting herself at risk too."

Larry drew his lips tight and looked at Chloe, who mirrored his expression and then raised her eyebrows.

Jim continued. "First, I've got some findings from the culture survey that I want to share with you because I think they link to the productivity problems Chloe says you're having. Then I'd like to talk about the three-sixty feedback I collected, and how it relates to the culture-assessment findings. Whether it helps you or not, though, is up to you."

Larry turned to Chloe and said impatiently, "If you think I'm not getting the productivity I need, then increase my budget so I can pay people enough to motivate them, or pay what it takes to get better people." Then, clenching his teeth, he remembered how Macon had mentioned saying the same thing in his ill-fated meeting with the boss.

Chloe, with a pained tightening of her lips, appeared to be about to engage Larry on that point. But instead, she said calmly yet firmly, "We can talk about the budget later. I think our time now would be better spent on Jim's feedback."

"Well, then, Jim, hit me with your best shot," Larry said,

letting out a deep breath. He resolved to do a better job watching what he let slip.

Jim nodded, seemingly unbothered by the brief spike of tension in the room. "Okay. Pull up a chair and let's take a look at these results."

They all sat at Chloe's conference table. Jim passed Larry a sheet of paper containing a multicolored wheel-shaped diagram. "You've seen this circumplex before, right?" he asked.

"Sure, every year for the past four years, I think. Same picture, same story, better than some companies, not as good as others," Larry droned, and sighed wearily. "So what's new this year?"

"Well, in the past, you looked at this diagram from the point of view of an individual on a team. But this year, Larry, the picture I'm showing you is a picture of *your* team, and by direct correlation, your leadership. Think of it as an X-ray."

"Of what?"

"The perception others have of your leadership and its effects. See, in the past, you saw pictures of a team on which you were a member, so while it captured your individual input, you never had the level of responsibility or span of control to isolate your impact on others. This year, though, you're the guy who's responsible for shaping the culture you've got there in front of you. So it's really a lot more important for you to see what it's telling you. Take a minute to look at it, and tell me what you see."

Larry looked. He didn't need to be a statistician to read

what was in front of him. He knew plenty about inter-
preting numbers. But to take them seriously, he had to believe in the value of these numbers, and he wasn't sure he
did. Nevertheless, he considered the picture.

It was a circle divided up into areas labeled with words
like "vision," "empowerment," teamwork," "concern for
people," and other indexes that purported to measure the
culture of his group. For each area, there was a number in-
dicating the strength of the measure, according to the per-
ceptions of the people who had answered the survey.

Larry looked at the number of responses for his group:
Ninety-six percent of the people who worked for him had
completed the survey. He knew enough about sampling
to see that he couldn't challenge the validity of these findings on the basis of response rate.

And what the people on Larry's team told him, with no
room for doubt, was that in the areas of "empowerment,"
"vision," "communication," and "associate development,"
there was strong and unanimous dissatisfaction.

Larry's pained expression prompted Jim to speak, trying to lighten Larry's mood by directing him to some
strengths: "You'll have some time to look at the details
later. You'll find it's not all bad news, by the way. Everyone
agrees that in your group it's clear that there are high
standards for output. You can take credit for setting high
expectations for productivity, effort, and initiative. Your
team members also agree that you're clearly goal-driven,
that you value safety, and that you promote strong bias
for action."

Larry nodded with some satisfaction. *That's good,* he

thought. *My people know what I expect, and they know I expect a lot. I must be getting through to them. Who said my communication skills need work?*

". . . the areas that seem to be causing trouble," Jim was saying as Larry tuned back in, "relate to your team's feeling that they don't *know* specifically what all their efforts add up to. They know you've got goals, but they see those as short-term goals for pieces of the project. They're not certain about your long-term goals for them or the business."

Larry reflected, *True. And they don't need to. That's my concern. They just need to focus on their sewing and let me worry about the quilt.*

Jim turned a page in the report and pointed to another chart. "They don't indicate any feelings of ownership for your group's work."

Ownership, Larry thought, fighting an impulse to close his eyes and massage his temples. *Give me a break. They don't own the company. They've got jobs here that they were hired to do. They want ownership, let 'em go out and buy stock!*

"Over here," Jim said, touching an area of a bar chart, "they indicate substantial dissatisfaction with the level of support they're getting from you in developing in their roles. People tend to think you see them as little more than hired hands . . . "

Well-paid ones, too.

". . . these are serious issues for you. They boil down to three areas. Your people want to *know* where they're going. They want to feel like partners in getting there, and they want to *own* the outcomes. And they want to *grow* on the journey. And they're telling you that, as far as they're concerned, your job is to help them with those things. They want, in short, less micromanagement and more empowering leadership."

Larry shifted in his chair, alternately sitting up straight and leaning forward, then leaning back and slumping, finding it hard to get comfortable as he listened to Jim. Leading this project was the first time he'd come under such scrutiny, and he felt himself buckling under this new weight of others' expectations. Why did they want him to use skills that he honestly didn't think mattered? Larry had always been able to rely on his intelligence and technical expertise, his can-do attitude—but now everyone was saying that wasn't enough.

Chloe and Jim had a lot to say, but they didn't have to do his job. On top of that, Larry began questioning their assumptions: *Who's to say these things ultimately make a difference? Sure, you found what your surveys measure, but can you prove that any of it matters? Consultants love to measure the things they have an answer for. This guy wants to sell his brand of leadership training, so he measures the things he calls leadership. It's all pretty self-serving, if you ask me. I can't believe Chloe spends the company's money on this.*

Inwardly rejecting what Jim was telling him, and finding what he considered to be a reasonable and intelligent way of doing so, Larry felt somewhat relieved. Still, though, something vague gnawed at him. He couldn't help but think about Macon's fall from grace.

And so, remembering Macon's advice about fending off Chloe, and hearing Jim finish talking, Larry said, "I know I can do a better job with empowering people, delegating responsibility, leveraging the diversity of opinions on my team. It's just that with the project timeline and budget in jeopardy, it's hard to let go. The risk is just too great."

"Larry, your company's paying me to be honest with you. And that's what I'm doing," Jim continued. "You're a smart guy. No one disputes that. And you know it, too. But lately, you're faking it. You faked your way through my workshop, and you're trying to fake it with your team. You know all the clichés about empowerment, dignity, and concern for people, and you can give the right answers, as you just demonstrated. But in your actions, you deliver a contrary message. You occasionally mouth phrases like, 'Everyone has a valuable contribution to make to the team,' and, 'Mistakes should be viewed as opportunities for learning and improvement.' But when anyone on your team makes a mistake, you attack, and then you take over and do that person's job."

Larry felt a need to defend himself: "What you say may be true, but under the kind of pressure this project has developed, I can't always be bothered with niceties. You know, sometimes a well-timed scowl of disapproval can change someone's behavior a whole lot quicker than a month's worth of coaching. These people are all grown-ups. I don't have the time to worry about hurt feelings. We've got some aggressive targets to hit. Plus, it's not like we're planning a manned mission to Mars here. If my people don't know where we're going or how we're getting there, why don't they ask?"

"That's a great question, Larry," Jim countered. "I think it's one *you* need to answer. What is it about the way you interact with them that keeps them from asking about direction? Could it be your use of the *well-timed scowl*, for example?"

It works with my kids, Larry said privately. Taking a deep breath, he puffed his cheeks, then let out the air in a rush. "I don't know." He tilted his head back and looked at the ceiling for an answer, or an escape route. "I don't know."

"I'm sorry to be putting you on the spot, Larry. I know that being confronted is uncomfortable. But no one's paying me to sugarcoat the message. Your company has values that aren't just words on paper. They've been given a lot of thought, and your company has invested time and money in determining the behaviors that support those values.

"*Empowerment*, for example, doesn't just mean telling someone else that he's responsible and then walking away, only to return later and take over when he messes up, or take it for granted if he succeeds. But look, I can see by your expression that this is becoming uncomfortable for you, and we can always go back to the details later. So I'll get to the nitty-gritty."

Jim held up Chloe's copy of the latest status report on the Singapore project. "These numbers are your wake-up call. When a project's in trouble, people look to the boss for leadership. They need more than just a technical expert. They've got plenty of technical expertise themselves, though many of them are so stressed at this point that they're not even using those abilities as well as they might."

Larry wanted to break in and tell this guy, *This is all easy for you to say. You don't have to answer for my goals. You just waltz in here, do your guru thing, then go home and prepare the bill. Meanwhile, I've got a bunch of cats to herd!* But he remembered Macon's warning about how Chloe wanted this kind of meeting to go, and so he kept quiet.

"If your leadership was working," Jim went on, "then these numbers would be improving. When you review the three-sixty feedback I've got here, you'll see that it's not just about project numbers. Your people are telling you that it's about *leadership*. Your single-pointed focus on what you need to do to get output today without concern for *how* you go about getting it is actually *hurting* that output, and your team is falling apart in the bargain.

"Without going into the painful details of who said what and who did what to whom, one of your team members did mention a situation a couple of weeks ago in one of your team meetings when, according to him, a problem-solving session broke down into finger-pointing, one of your team members threatened to quit, and all you offered was a look of disgust and a warning to—" Jim consulted his notes, " 'grow up, or find yourselves a new playground,' when what they needed was someone to step in, provide a model for them of how to resolve the conflict, and guide them in coming up with an action plan.

"Larry, you've got an orchestra full of talented musicians. Help them to understand the music you've put in front of them. Help them to *hear* it, and then inspire them to play it like they've never played it before. You can't play all the instruments and still conduct the symphony. And even if you could, what would any of the people in the orchestra learn that would help you improve their next performance?"

Jim went silent, calmly awaiting a reply. *Finally, a chance to talk*, Larry thought. He took a breath and said, "Dammit, Jim, I brought in a process consultant to work with the core team to help them sort out the process issues. He spent a whole day interviewing them one by one, then another day with them as a group. According to him, they did great work together. But the team hasn't changed *anything* as a result. They're still going around like a bunch of chickens with their heads cut off. If I had the chance, I'd replace three-quarters of them."

"You're making excuses. You refer to your team as *them*, not us. Larry, let me ask you this, though I know the answer: Did *you* attend that session with the process consultant?"

"You know I didn't," Larry said, defiance in his voice and narrowing eyes. "I planned to, but then I had a crisis to deal with when one of our suppliers declared bankruptcy."

"Larry, listen to yourself: 'I planned to, but . . . ' 'It's not my fault.' Excuses! 'I'm doing my job—why won't people leave me alone?' Baloney. Look, Larry. When you just said you'd replace three-quarters of your team if you could—"

"Well, maybe I spoke out of frustration," Larry interrupted.

"The thing is, several of your people told me they thought that's exactly what you *would* do. They're looking for leadership, and just about all they're getting is criticism. And they believe that's why the project's in trouble. In fact, a few of them said they would leave your team voluntarily if they could do that without harming their careers here."

Larry felt his stomach clench. "Well, good riddance. If they don't get on the stick and start doing their jobs, they won't have a career here anyway. No one hired me to be a baby-sitter. I've told these people what I want them to do. I don't understand why they won't just do it and leave me alone so that I can manage this project." He stood up, his face reddening and throat constricting.

"Have a seat, Larry. I'm the one who needs to leave soon. And I want to leave on a thoughtful note. Here's what I hear you saying: You tell your people what to do, then you want them to go do it and leave you alone. Have I gotten that right?"

"Yep. That's pretty much it."

"Does that describe what it means to be a leader?"

Larry tilted his head up and thrust his jaw forward a little. "Go ask Patton," he said.

Chloe stepped in to thank Jim Enos for his time and see him to the door. As Larry sat waiting for her to return, he felt his shoulders slumping. He couldn't take his eyes off the table.

"Suck it up, Larry," Chloe said as she sat down close beside him. She was trying to be reassuring, he could tell. "You're one of the smartest people I know. Not to mention one of the most stubborn. Use that intelligence and stubbornness to *change* your behavior. You can pull this off. The project needs the knowledge and technical skills you bring to it. If you can find the way to master *how* you bring that expertise to the team and figure out a way to involve your people more fully in getting results, you can still turn this around. We're *counting* on you, but time is of the essence now."

She gathered the pages of the three-sixty report and went on: "But, Larry, you need to recognize that your people are not the problem. We hire the best people in the field. These folks are used to success. Like you, maybe some have even been a little spoiled by it. A good leader can bring this back on course, and I still believe you can be that leader."

Not encouraged, but trying to find some consolation in Chloe's words, Larry managed a tepid, "Thanks."

"Anyway," Chloe continued, looking Larry in the eyes, "with the delay in the schedule resulting from the permits problem in Singapore and the Farnum bankruptcy, I think this is an ideal time for you to take some time away from the office. I've confirmed it with Bob Passentino in HR. We won't count it against your vacation time. Just get away from this, do some reflecting, relax and recharge. Think about what you're going to do differently, and come up with a plan to focus on *leadership*.

"That's your assignment. I'll help temporarily with project oversight. It'll give us all a chance to regroup. Only thing is, if you decide to go anywhere, let me know how to get in touch with you in case something critical comes up that I can't handle."

With a bitter smile of disbelief, Larry said, "What you're really telling me is that I need to give my *team* a break, aren't you?"

"That's *not* what I'm saying, Larry. What I am saying is that *you* need a break from the day-by-day, minute-by-minute action so that you can step back, see the bigger picture, and come to the right decision. Which is that this project is going to turn around and succeed only if you change your leadership of it."

Larry decided he wasn't going to get anywhere with someone who clearly didn't understand what it meant to manage this project. He decided to give in. Maybe managing the day-to-day crises will open Chloe's eyes, he thought. He told her, "Okay, I understand. I could use a few days with Jessie and the kids anyway. I've neglected them lately. Just one thing, though: If it hadn't been for Enos's *findings*"—he made little quotation marks in the air with both hands as he emphasized the word—"would I still be getting this bonus vacation?"

Chloe put her hand to her square chin for a moment as she summoned a response. "It's not really a *vacation*, Larry, because you have an assignment, which is to come back and tell me how you're going to lead your team. But of course, you can do whatever you want with your time."

"Whatever," Larry said, glumly.

"Do you remember when you once told me, with no

disguising your contempt, that, 'A consultant is someone who asks to borrow your watch, tells you the time, then charges you for the information'?"

"Yeah," Larry said, and blew a sigh. "I remember."

"Well, Larry, you just got told what time it is."

CHAPTER EIGHT

Have Fun

"Home so early, Dad?" Jennifer said when Larry came through the kitchen door.

"After six isn't really *early*, is it?" Larry said.

"Since you took on *The Project*," Jennifer answered, emphasizing the words like the name of a monster in a horror movie, "early is anytime before everyone else has finished eating." Her pretty face was troubled by a frown. "Sometimes it's just in time to say goodnight."

"I know, honey. Well, for now that will change, since *Dad's been given an extra vacation*," he said, elevating his voice to feign cheerfulness.

Jennifer's blue eyes widened. "Have you been canned?"

"No, sweetheart, I haven't been *canned*," Larry said quickly, trying to instill his voice with more confidence than he felt. "What it means is I'm being rewarded for working so hard with some well-deserved time off. A chance to rest up."

At that moment Jessie and David finished setting out a

dinner of roasted chicken, rice pilaf, salad, corn bread, and French-style green beans.

Dinners at the Parks house—at least when Larry was home—often involved spirited conversations about the events of each person's day. Tonight was only slightly different, with Larry preferring to keep to himself what had happened at the office in order to focus on David and Jennifer.

Jennifer spoke about her plans for summer camp, now only a couple of months away, and Larry was temporarily won over by the musical quality of her voice as she anticipated the trouble that she and her best friend, Elizabeth, would give their counselors.

David talked, as always, about baseball. Tall and lean and sinewy, he bent over his plate, wolfing down fork after fork of "great grub," as he called it. Between mouthfuls he boasted about how he was getting the knack of readjusting to the low breaking ball and "going to the opposite field with it." Larry nodded approvingly, inviting his son to elaborate in greater detail.

"Coach says it's all about visualizing where you want the ball to land, and then going with the flow. He told me to stop using the bat as a weapon and start thinking about it as an extension of my arms. It's helped me to make my swing more organic."

"*Organic flow.* I'm impressed," Jessie said. "That's good advice for life, not just baseball. Your coach must be a wise man."

"Guess so," David said, shrugging. "Coach also talks about how players contribute more than just hits and putouts. He coaches us on the things that don't show up on the box score, like how we cheer for each other, celebrate each other's successes. Sure is better than that drill sergeant I had in Little League. He acted like his future depended on winning the West Side championship."

"I'm proud of you that you appreciate that," Jessie replied. "I wish I could say the same thing for all those over-involved parents sitting like a bunch of jacks-in-the-box in the stands yelling at their kids about keeping their head down and their eye on the ball." When she looked at Larry, he couldn't tell whether she was being accusatory or merely hoping for some agreement.

"Sports can teach some good lessons," Larry said, finding himself getting irritated at the way the conversation was going. "Still, at your age and level, your coach can't overemphasize mechanics. Bad habits are hard to break later on. The recruiters are looking at form as much as anything else—well, except for numbers. And don't kid yourself: Stats more than anything will get you a scholarship. Batting average. Slugging percentage. RBIs. Errors."

"Here we go!" David said, turning to Jennifer and lifting his eyes toward the ceiling.

"Joke all you want, hotshot," Larry said, his voice tense now. "Sure, the colleges want kids with a healthy perspective on the game. But more than that, they want kids who will fill the trophy cases in the alumni club, raise the level of their program, make it attractive to recruits and donors. And at the end of the day, the numbers you put up are what separates the winners from the losers. Winners don't need to content themselves with talk about moral victories, 'cause they have *real* wins in the record book."

"Geez, Dad," Jennifer interrupted. "*Lighten up*—it's just high school baseball. This is getting a little heavy for my taste. Can I be excused?" She stood up.

"Not until we're all done," Larry answered sharply.

Blushing, Jennifer challenged, "Well, *aren't* we?"

Larry looked around at the empty plates. In a voice filled with a sudden exhausted resignation, he said, "I guess so. David, Jenn, I want you to clear the dishes tonight. I need to go talk to your mom about some things." He got up and lumbered out of the room. Jessie followed, putting her hand on the small of his tired back.

In their oversized bedroom, its walls a soothing light salmon color, Larry and Jessie sat on a small couch facing each other.

Jessie's green eyes narrowed as she studied Larry's face. "So what's eating you tonight? As if I didn't know. And what's this I hear about a vacation?"

Larry looked out the window, consciously avoiding eye contact. "There's a delay in the project. Chloe says it's a time for me to rest and reflect. She calls it 'sharpening the blade.' But I'm not so sure."

"*Why*, Larry? Do you have any reason to think she'd mislead you?"

"She's my boss!" Larry answered. "Of course she'd keep things from me. That's what bosses *do*!"

"Do they *all*?" Jessie asked, pulling her dark blond hair behind her ears.

"Well, look," Larry said. "This is exactly what she did to Macon. Going to the guys he works with to get feedback, sending him off to Enos's *workshop*, then an extended troubleshooting assignment, then a *vacation*. This is just how it started with *him*." Larry's voice rose in agitation. "Next thing you know, I'll be troubleshooting some installation in Argentina for three months while someone else takes over Singapore.

"But Macon came back, didn't he?" asked Jessie. "They *invested* in him with all those things. Just like they're doing with you now. If Chloe's lying to you, would she be wasting company money on your development, or paying you to take a vacation? Don't you think she's smart enough to have learned a lesson with Macon? She must see some differences between the two of you."

"Yeah, maybe," Larry admitted. "But sometimes I think she's just doing what someone above her tells her to do, or else doing what she knows will impress the CEO. She's so political that I think the only reason she does anything is because she thinks it will advance her standing in the company. I'm amazed you don't recognize that, after everything I've told you about her." In the back of his mind somewhere, Larry knew he was being unfair to Jessie and, probably, to Chloe as well. But he wasn't in a mood to turn off the dark road he was traveling.

"Surely you don't think she'd spend money on Macon's training just to make herself look good, do you?" Jessie challenged. "What *happened* when Macon came back to work after his vacation? Had he changed?"

"No, he hadn't. And why should he? Macon's the *best* at what he does. He could manage circles around Chloe."

"Managing *what*? Surely you can't mean people, Larry. Macon's so clearly old-school. He doesn't trust anyone. And now that we're talking about it, it's always worried me a little that you chose him as a mentor. I know he's got a lot to offer related to engineering, but how could he possibly help you with leadership?"

"What are you talking about?" Larry said irritably. "Whose side are you on?"

"I'm on *your* side, Larry. I can't believe you don't know that," Jessie said, hurt in her voice and eyes. "It's just that sometimes being on your side means I feel like I need to confront you. Because, as brilliant as you are, you're that stubborn and that hard to change."

"Now *you* sound just like Chloe. Why isn't being smart and being good at my job enough?"

"Maybe it's because now you've got a *new* job," Jessie offered.

"Dammit, Jessie. You sound like Chloe *and* that jerk Enos. I don't need to be hammered at home, too. I'm just looking for a little understanding and support. You know?"

Jessie's face darkened as she stood up. "Come on, Larry, that's unfair. I don't know whether to feel hurt for you or be insulted that you're so badly misreading my intentions. I'm not trying to criticize you. I'm trying to help you see what you're missing. And I have to admit, too, that I and the kids are feeling like we play second fiddle lately. You know, just about every night since you started this project, you come home late, and then unload your burdens. On weekends when you could be helping around the house, or going to David's ballgames, you're in the office trying to catch up. Larry, I hate that you hate your job and that you spend so little time with us."

Offended and defensive, Larry stammered, "I—I don't know what to say. I didn't realize I was being such a pain around here. Maybe it would be a good idea if I took a couple of days to get away. I don't know, maybe do some fishing—you know, try to figure this out." A tone of despair started to color his voice.

"Where would you go?" Jessie asked.

Larry heard worry in her voice, a tone he recognized from times when she spoke with concern about the kids. But he felt he couldn't do anything but answer her question: "I remember Macon saying he had the use of a fishing cabin somewhere not too far from here. Maybe I could use that."

"Well, if you think that would do you some good, and let you return more relaxed so you could enjoy being with us, I guess I'm all for it. Only, do me a favor, honey, okay?"

"What's that, Jess?"

"Have fun, but also use the time to think about how you're going to turn this thing around."

Larry tightened his lips somewhat sheepishly. "I hear you, sweetheart," he said. "I'll go call Macon now."

CHAPTER NINE

Follow the Leader

"So, it's Larry the Conqueror," Macon said, an odd tone in his voice that Larry couldn't interpret. "Good to hear from you, I guess. Is this the requisite sympathy call?"

"What in the world are you talking about, Macon?"

"Don't *tell* me you haven't heard the *news*," the older man challenged.

"What news?"

"Chloe canned me this afternoon."

"You're kidding!"

"No, I am not kidding. But if you're not calling about that, then what's up?"

"Oh, Macon, I'm almost embarrassed to ask now. I was calling to ask about that fishing cabin you've got access to."

"Well, coincidence of coincidences," said Macon, his voice brightening. "That just happens to be where I'm headed. If you'd called twenty minutes later, you'd have missed me, 'cause I'm off for a couple of days of fishing."

"Got room for a fishing buddy?"

"Absolutely. Meet me out at the 7-Eleven on 835—you know where that is. You can follow me out to the lake."

Larry suggested taking one car, but Macon explained that after the fishing he was headed off in the opposite direction to visit his brother, who happened to be a lawyer, to review the terms of his severance. So Larry loaded his gear into his car, told David and Jennifer he was going fishing for a couple of days, kissed Jessie goodbye, and drove off to meet his mentor.

As he drove to the 7-Eleven, reflecting on the bad turns at work, Larry replayed bits of conversation he'd had with Jessie over the past few days:

"You know, during those couple of years I worked for the vocational-counseling service, I heard it over and over from my clients who were considering new careers—that their bosses only watched the bottom line and didn't care how they got there. I remember one of them saying that he honestly believed his boss viewed him as 'collateral damage.'

"Why does it have to be a one-or-the-other situation for you, Larry? Why can't you have it both ways—care about the bottom line and also care about your people? Why aren't those connected for you?" Jessie had challenged him one evening after a late dinner.

"I *do* care about my people," he'd defended himself. "I show it every day by checking up on them, making sure they're doing their assignments."

———

"You know, Larry," she'd said after a particularly unpleasant end to a recent family dinner, "if you treat your team the way you treat your kids, it's no wonder things are going badly."

"What do you mean?" Larry had snapped back. "When people do something wrong, they need to be corrected. And what Jennifer did was just flat-out wrong. You don't blow off a major assignment at school and then lie about it."

"Maybe so, Larry," Jessie had said, trying to calm him. "But alternately ignoring someone and then criticizing her isn't the way to change behavior. Maybe she hid the truth because she knew how you'd react to it. Anyway, I think Jenn's just trying to get some attention from you, and maybe this is the only way she knows how to get it."

"Well she's got it now, hasn't she?" he snorted.

"I'm afraid to say she has," Jessie had answered. "I'll bet she wishes it would go away."

On top of those distracting voices in his head, Larry felt a low, deep pang of guilt gnawing at him about leaving his family so soon after coming home. He was glad when he reached the 7-Eleven and found Macon waiting for him. Anything to take his mind off all this.

"I can't believe she fired you," Larry offered.

"Bull. I bet you saw it coming. She's been gunning for me for two years now. Guess she finally got her excuse."

"What's that?"

"Ah, some supplier complained to the project lead that

he wouldn't do any more work for KGO if he had to interact with me."

"Man! What did you do to him?"

"The guy didn't care about quality, so I let him know what I thought of him. Seemed fair to me. Let's go inside and get some coffee."

As they walked in and drained the coffeepot that stood next to the front counter, Macon went on.

"She had other grudges against me, and mumbled something about quarterly profits being off from a beating we took on the Orlando installation. Then comes the pile driver: She tells me the company is committed to embracing 'a new direction in leadership development and culture,' and it's pretty clear I intend to be an obstacle to moving that way. Can you believe that?"

"So what did you say?" Larry asked. He started to feel a vague burden in having had his own career linked so closely to Macon's—especially now that they seemed to be following the same path.

"It kept going downhill from there. I confronted her. I demanded that she show me one piece of evidence that I wasn't doing my job to the best of my ability. Which between you and me and this fine display of potato chips, we all know is plenty of ability. I told her to get my performance reviews and show me where I wasn't hitting or exceeding my goals!" Larry noticed that Macon's face was flushed; a prominent vein pulsed in his forehead. He started to worry about his friend's blood pressure.

"So what did Chloe say?" Larry asked.

"The strangest thing, really, that she's ever said to me,"

Macon answered, his tone full of genuine wonder. "She told me, 'Macon, you're *not* doing your job. You're only doing part of it. I've been trying to help you to understand this for at least the past two review cycles.' That's when it started to turn ugly. Meanwhile, that dimwitted HR slug, Passentino, is just sitting there at the table taking notes, waiting for his turn to disclose the generous terms of my severance."

"Passentino's not so bad," Larry said, feeling a need to defend the HR man for reasons that puzzled him.

"Not so bad!" Macon challenged, screwing up his mouth and nose. "Whose side are you on? Have you finally become brainwashed?"

Sorry now to have said something that apparently caused Macon to feel betrayed, Larry shrugged and said, "Anyway, how did you respond to them?"

"I said, 'So, if I'm not doing all of my job, why haven't you defined for me before this what the rest of my job *is*?' I never saw anything in my performance plan that said I had to mollycoddle my people."

"And then?" Larry prompted, his mouth getting dry.

"Get this. Chloe tells me, 'Macon, I've told you in so many words, again and again. I sent you to training seminars. I got you three-sixty-degree feedback. You told me you thought I was doing that to punish you, but I did that to try to help.'" Macon forced a self-conscious laugh. And Larry felt a jolt up his spine, realizing he'd suggested much the same thing to Chloe about his own experience.

Macon suggested that Larry pay for their coffee: "Seems only fair, since you still have a job, plus you're getting a free fishing vacation to boot," Macon said, and Larry thought he heard a trace of bitterness in his tone.

Larry cleared his throat and said, "Macon, I'm really sorry."

"Don't worry about me, Larry. Probably one of the best things that ever happened to me. There's a world of opportunity out there for an engineering consultant to make a fortune helping incompetents with the technical aspects of their jobs. I'll be just fine."

"Glad to hear it," Larry said, sensing that Macon was either putting up a false front or hadn't really come to grips with his situation. He'd spent decades of his life at KGO, and he hated to fail at anything he tried. But to change the subject, Larry asked, "So where are we headed?"

"Just follow me," Macon said, looking west as the last light faded. "We'll be there before you know it. I hear the best time to fish for walleye on this lake is after dark."

"You mean we're gonna fish *tonight*? I was thinking we could have a beer, talk a little, get to bed early, and fish in the morning."

"We can drink and talk while we fish, and then we can fish some *more* in the morning. And we're wasting time standing around here talking." Macon walked quickly to his car. "Just follow me. And see if you can keep up, my boy."

Soon Larry followed Macon's car off the brightly lit highway and started winding down a dark country road, just barely wide enough for its two lanes. As Macon sped ahead in the dark, Larry chuckled at how his old mentor seemed to view even driving down a rural road as a sort of competition, a survival of the fittest.

But three stressful miles later, as Macon continued to lengthen his distance in front of Larry and turned onto yet another unmarked and even narrower potholed road, Larry's sense of humor stretched beyond breaking. He complained to the dark, "What the hell is the rush?"

Larry tried to calm himself, wanting to give Macon the benefit of the doubt and feeling momentarily guilty for his anger. Maybe the guy was so preoccupied with losing his job that he couldn't think about the difficulty of trying to follow him. Or maybe he resented how Larry had taken over the Singapore project and still worked at the old company.

A few minutes later, though, when Larry lost sight of Macon's taillights completely, he gave up trying to excuse his friend's behavior. He had bigger things to think about, skidding around a sharp turn and coming to yet another branch in the road. Larry hit the brakes hard and stopped, trying to guess which road to take.

"Dammit!" Larry cursed himself for driving off on this fool's mission. He was now lost in the woods, without a compass, map, or even a flashlight. "I can't believe I'd follow a crazy man into the dark without knowing where we're going!" Then, hearing the irony in what he'd just said, he added, "I guess it'd be even stupider to follow a crazy man if I *did* know where we were going."

Pulling onto the road's soft shoulder, Larry decided to

call Macon on his cell phone. He couldn't imagine his friend turning around to get him, but at least he could say which branch of the road to take. But Macon wasn't answering his phone.

"Why in the world couldn't he have told me where we were going? Why didn't I insist on a map or some directions?" Larry cried out to the night.

He considered turning around and trying to retrace his path back out of the woods. But he'd been trusting Macon so completely that he hadn't paid any attention to their route. If he drove back, Larry feared, he could easily take a wrong turn and only get further lost. Then he'd lose any chance of Macon's coming back and finding him. He dialed Macon's number again. The phone was still off.

"Where *is* that jerk?" Larry screamed. He couldn't believe that Macon hadn't even realized that he'd lost the car behind him.

He remembered something Macon had once told him: "When in doubt, always go to the right." He decided to drive down that branch of the road in hopes of finding his way.

This is just the way the guy was to work for, Larry thought as he squinted ahead through the light of his high beams. *Always playing follow-the-leader and taking off on a path to only-he-knew-where, never checking to see if anyone was still with him. It's no wonder the company fired him. I can just imagine what his consulting business'll be like. I bet he'll create more problems for his clients than he solves!*

Larry's bitter thoughts about Macon gave way to bitter

thoughts about work. His team seemed to be moving aim-lessly in the dark in all different directions. That was just how he felt now, feeling his way in a moonless night, hear-ing only the grating, metallic chirp of crickets and the oc-casional hoot of an owl.

Suddenly, Larry swerved to avoid hitting a young doe that sprang out of the bushes just as he came around a turn. After momentarily freezing, it bounded away, but Larry ended up hopelessly stuck in a ditch just over the shoulder of the road.

He smacked the steering wheel with both hands. Then he regained his composure and admitted to himself that he was stuck where he was until morning unless by some stroke of luck someone came along. He turned on his car radio and found a talk show to keep himself company. Two child psychologists were debating the merits of the "tough love" approach to discipline. But hearing the talk about children renewed Larry's stirrings of guilt about choosing to go fishing when he could have been home with his family. He hit more radio buttons until he found a call-in show about the possibilities of extraterrestrial life, which was absurd enough to distract him.

Larry listened until he fell into fitful sleep. In his dreams, he was trying to dig his way through a pitch-black tunnel. He could hear a voice up ahead beckoning, "Come on, my boy, only a few more miles." And from be-hind he could hear several voices: "Who the heck dug this hole?" "We've got to fill in this hole before someone falls in!" "This hole's not supposed to be *here*, the customer wanted it over *there* . . ."

Larry felt the air grow hotter. Drops of sweat ran down his forehead and stung his eyes. He found it almost impossible to breathe and began to panic as he heard shovels of earth being dumped behind him.

"Hey, I'm *in* here!" he yelled. "There's someone *in* here!"

Then a voice as calm as Jim Enos's whispered, "You're just below the surface. Digging down will only get you in deeper. Change direction and dig straight up. You can do it."

"But I don't know which way is up," Larry confessed. *What happened to gravity?* Nothing he took for granted could help him. "I can't breathe—they're burying me!" He felt his mouth fill with dirt.

CHAPTER TEN

Lost

Larry awoke hyperventilating and clammy, feeling as though he were suffocating. Disoriented as first light came through his windshield, he breathed more calmly as he remembered where he was. The memory of what had happened the previous night left him dismayed, but he couldn't help feeling relieved at being awake.

Larry peered out his car windows, unable to see much with the early-morning fog hugging the ground. And he quickly understood that even if he could see the surroundings, he still wouldn't know where he was. He couldn't remember seeing any road signs the night before, either.

So this is what it means to be "lost in the woods," Larry thought, reflecting on how often he'd used that phrase to describe people who couldn't seem to find their way out of problems.

He picked up his cell phone to call a tow truck, but the battery was dead. Anyway, how could he even tell the auto club where to find him? And so, with no other apparent choice, and because he subscribed to the belief that doing something was always better than doing nothing, Larry got out of the car and walked.

Choosing a way to go really wasn't a tough call. Since he hadn't passed anything for quite a while on his journey to this point, he went forward rather than back, reasoning that even though he didn't know what was ahead, he knew there was nothing behind him within walking distance.

Walking on the gravel alongside the road, Larry noticed the increasing volume and variety of birds chirping as the sun rose. It sounded to him as though the birds were involved in a big argument, everyone talking at once and no one listening. *Is this what one of our team meetings would sound like to an outside observer?* he thought. Then he snorted, realizing how even his appreciation of nature was being tainted by his work.

Larry made his way through intermittent swarms of insects and kept walking straight ahead, resisting turnoffs at various points along the way for fear he wouldn't be able to trace his way back if he decided at some point to turn around. He guessed he must have walked at least four miles when he came to a small bait shop—the only kind of store that would be open so early in the day.

A sign was painted on a weathered cedar shingle that read: "You can bring your smokes inside, but leave the burdens and bull out here." An arrow on it pointed down to an old commode on the ground.

Entering, he almost choked on the cigar smoke, clouding the air even worse than the morning fog.

"Good morning," he said to the two gray-haired, flannel-shirted men who sat behind a counter next to a large metal tank full of minnows. They were playing cards, gin rummy by the look of it.

"Morning," said one, blowing out a plume of smoke. "Whatcha need?" He plugged the cigar back into the corner of his mouth, clenched between his teeth.

"Help is what I need first," Larry said. "My car's in a ditch a few miles back, and I need to call someone to tow it. Can I use your phone?"

The man pointed to a black dial phone on the counter. "Help yourself," he mumbled, moving his lips no more than a ventriloquist.

Laconic fellow, Larry thought. But somehow there was power in those two words, if he could get a handle on what it was. "Thanks. Only thing is, I don't know where I am."

"Ahhh. Walt's. And if you want a guy with a tow truck who knows just where that is, you can call Jerry. Card's over there on that wall." The man with the cigar pointed to a cork board hanging under a huge mounted walleye. "You got triple A? Jerry's got a contract with 'em. Save you some money."

"That's great. I really appreciate it," Larry said.

"No cost to me," the man said, turning back to his hand and laying it down like a fan. "Gin!"

While he waited for Jerry to arrive with his tow truck, Larry watched the game of cards, browsed around the shack, and admired the small but worthy assortment of rods, reels, and lures. This was a tackle shop for the serious fisherman, Larry thought. That led him to ask, "Do either of you know a guy named Macon? I think maybe he fishes around here."

"Dunno," said the one counting the unmatched cards in his hand. "What's he look like?"

"Gray, stubbly hair, about five-eleven. Muscular build for a guy in his early fifties, but looks tired—you know, big bags under his eyes. Oh, and he drives a black four-by-four."

Both men looked up at Larry at the same time. The one with the cigar asked, "Kind of a know-it-all?"

"You could say that," Larry chuckled.

"Yep, we know 'im. Fact, he was in here before sunup, for bait. Thought his name was Dobbs."

"That's him. His first name's Macon," Larry said, feeling excitement rise at the prospect of finding his friend. But then it occurred to him: Macon wasn't looking for *him* at all. In fact, at this very moment he was somewhere on the lake fishing. Macon had ditched him. And apparently he'd *chosen* to do that—or he'd done it without caring, which was even worse.

Larry decided then and there that he'd spent too much time following a fool to nowhere. Despite his feelings of loyalty and sorrow for his friend, he resolved to end his relationship with Macon.

CHAPTER ELEVEN

The Travel Agent

Jerry arrived, took Larry back to his car, pulled the car back onto the road, and jumped the battery, which had run down after Larry had fallen asleep with the radio on. Finally, he sketched a map leading back to the main highway—Larry no longer had any wish to find Macon's cabin. After signing papers, he was on his way.

The only question was, *Where?*

Larry pondered that question as he turned down first one wooded road and then another, noting only the occasional cottage well off the road. Sometimes he wondered if Jerry's directions were correct. But every time he looked at the map, he could see that—sure enough—all those isolated twists and turns were adding up to the right direction. He spotted a subdivision, and then a road sign for a school crossing. *So at least I'm back in civilization*, he thought with some relief.

By the time Larry got back to the highway, early-morning traffic was picking up. School buses were making their rounds, and people were on their way to work, driving while talking on their cell phones.

Still unsure of his destination, Larry realized that the growl in his stomach wasn't only the gnawing of irritation and uncertainty. It was hunger. Never before had a Donut Castle looked so good.

Over coffee and a bagel, Larry reflected on how he might be welcomed if he went home. After all, he'd basically told his family that he preferred a few days with Macon and a boatload of fish to their company. How, then, could he return early and get back in everyone's good graces?

Larry was considering that question when, through the window of the donut shop, he noticed a large sign on the front of a new white building across the street. The words "Right Place–Right Time Travel Agency" painted beneath a bright orange sun against a blue sky and a white beach beckoned him to get away from it all. And that sounded good.

"Hi, I'm Lauren," the travel agent said, extending Larry a well-manicured hand. Her voice rising musically: "Thinking about a vacation? Or is it a business trip?" Her brow wrinkled a little as she eyed Larry's rumpled clothing and the thick shadow of his unshaven face.

"You'll need to forgive my appearance," Larry said. "I was supposed to be out fishing on a lake somewhere this morning, but I got lost in the woods last night and slept in my car."

"Then you definitely need to get away from it all. Although in this case, I guess it's really a matter of getting away from getting away, huh?" she laughed. "So, what did you have in mind?"

"Vacation, I guess. I'm here on impulse—I hadn't been thinking about it until I saw your sign. Although recently a couple of people have suggested I take a vacation." He laughed self-consciously, trying to break his tension.

"And what sort of vacation did you envision, umm . . . I didn't catch your name?"

"Oh, sorry, it's Larry. Larry Parks." He scanned the modern office and its travel posters inviting him to take on the challenge of golf in Bermuda, enjoy the amusements of Orlando, tour the fountains of Florence, indulge in the nightlife of Paris, surrender to the seductions of Rio, sail the verdant islands of Greece . . .

"Well then, Larry. What are you thinking about? And will you be taking your family?" Lauren asked, glancing at the gold wedding band on Larry's hand.

"Family, sure. But where? I haven't thought about that at all."

"So many choices," Lauren said sympathetically. "But what's your goal for this trip?"

Somewhat exhausted from his night in the woods, Larry's imagination failed him. He shrugged.

"Well, I hope it's to have fun." Lauren suggested. "But that's pretty general, and there are lots of different ways to achieve that. Sometimes, it helps some of my clients to think about what they'd like to be able to look back on afterward. You know, imagine yourself sitting with your family six months from now, and reminiscing about the great vacation you had together. What stories will you tell? Did you swim? Hike? Ride horses? Play golf? Tour museums? What kind of food did you eat? What sort of mementos did you bring home—a slipper full of pink sand? A piece of native pottery? What will you see in the photographs you all took?"

"Ah, I get it," Larry answered, starting to see something he couldn't quite yet define taking shape.

And then he planned the Parks family vacation.

PART TWO

CHAPTER TWELVE

"Know"

Driving home, Larry was refreshed just by the thought of getting away with his family. He imagined Jessie's surprise and delight when he told her where they were going and showed her the brochure. He thought about what Jennifer and David would say.

When he got home, he found Jessie in the attic, painting a still life of arranged wildflowers, a hobby she'd recently taken up now that their kids were becoming more independent.

"Hey, Jess," Larry said quietly, not wanting to disturb her but too eager to wait.

She turned with a start. "Oh, you scared me, Larry! I didn't expect you home today. What happened to the outing with Macon? And why do you look like you slept in your clothes?"

"Because I *did* sleep in my clothes. The whole thing was a sad fiasco, but it's behind me now and I'll tell you about it later. But listen, I've got a surprise."

"A good one, I hope," Jessie said cautiously.

"Guess where we're going next week," Larry coaxed.

"Out for a night of dining and dancing?"

"Bigger than that," he said, his excitement masking his weariness. "I made vacation plans. Since I have this time off, I figured we might as well use it to have some fun."

"Vacation plans?" Jessie said, much less thrilled than Larry had hoped. "*When?* And what sort of vacation?"

"Guess," Larry said.

"I wish I didn't have to, Larry. I like to be involved in these kinds of decisions."

Larry took the slim brochure out of his back pocket and held it out. Its cover said, "Find Your Bliss on Anguila." Jessie thumbed through the bright color photos of crystal white beaches dotted with rainbow umbrellas, people dancing on a veranda under the stars to a calypso band, spacious rooms decorated in rattan and shades of coral. But the first picture that really caught her eye showed a man in a fishing chair, his rod and arms straining against the pull of a sailfish suspended in midair off in the distance, while his wife and two teenage children looked on in glee. Jessie's eyes widened and then, looking up at Larry, narrowed. Her lips tightened.

"What is this?" she said, her voice signaling annoyance.

"That's where we're going. It's an island in the Caribbean."

"But who's *we*? You and Macon?"

"No. Us. You, me, the kids." Larry was starting to feel as if he'd run off the road again, this time smashing through a guardrail. "I stopped at the travel agent on the way home this morning and made plans."

"For a vacation," Jessie said. "By the looks of it, a vacation of deep-sea fishing off the coast of some remote island. Okay. I get it." She nodded. "And when did you decide we'd be doing this?"

"Next week," Larry answered cheerfully.

"Next week," Jessie repeated, shaking her head now from side to side. She sat on a small couch by the attic window.

"What's wrong?" Larry asked, going to sit next to her on the couch. He was beginning to feel hurt as well as confused. "I thought you'd be excited. A chance to get away from everything for a little while. Be together with the kids. Get some sun, swim, do a little dancing in the evening." He tried to get her to share his vision.

"Not to mention fishing," Jessie added, looking out the window.

"Well, yeah," Larry admitted. "I thought David might like that."

Now Jessie turned toward Larry, anger flaring momentarily in her eyes, then softening.

"Tell me," she said, putting her hand on his. "When you were with the travel agent, did you for a moment stop to think about whether you might consult with me about this?"

"The agent suggested that," Larry reflected. "But I wanted it to be a surprise. What's wrong with that?"

"A surprise would be you coming home on time for dinner with your family for a whole week. Or maybe you even stopped along the way and bought me flowers. This goes way beyond surprise, Larry. It's more like thoughtlessness."

"But it'll be great for us to get away and have fun together as a family. Can't you see that?"

"I can. And I guess I should be touched by the sentiment. But listen. Aside from whether or not this vacation you've planned is even the kind of vacation I'd like right now—and I've got some doubts about that—going on a vacation like this is a big thing. It's a big expense; it takes planning and preparation. A vacation's supposed to bring us all closer, so it needs to be something that we not only all agree on, but all had a part in shaping."

Larry's head hung down, and he looked at the floor.

"Larry, don't get me wrong. I *like* it that you're decisive. It's one of the things I've always admired about you, and it makes me feel secure. But being decisive doesn't mean that you never need to involve other people in decisions. It doesn't mean you just call all the shots and expect everyone else to gratefully follow along. You know, you've been doing that a lot lately around here. And from what you've been telling me, part of your problem at work might stem from the same sort of behavior."

Larry let out a short, forced laugh.

"What's funny?" Jessie asked, looking in his eyes.

"I was just thinking about a joke Macon once told me, when he and Jean were fighting a lot before their breakup."

"I hope you don't think *we're* breaking up," Jessie said, pulling back a little.

"No, it's not that. It's just that sometimes, like now, I can identify with the joke."

"Well, so what is it?"

"Guess it's kind of sexist, but here goes: If a man's walking alone in the forest, talking to himself, and there's nobody around to hear him, is he still wrong?"

"Ha!" Jessie said. "I know it's a rhetorical question. But I'm going to give you the answer anyway. The truth is, if he's talking to himself about a decision that should involve other people, then yes, he's wrong."

Larry didn't know how to respond to that. Suddenly uncomfortable, he realized how badly he felt the need to shave and shower and get into fresh clothes.

"I hear you, Jess. But I'm feeling pretty grungy. Mind if I have a shower, and then we can work this through?"

"Sure, you go get cleaned up. I need to finish this part of my painting anyway, before I lose the idea."

The hot water pulsing from the shower massage soothed the kinks in Larry's neck. After drying off, he completed his ritual of shaving, stretching the skin of his face to pull the razor first in one direction, then its opposite, then a third, in his quest to get every last bit of stubble. He always had a hard time with the small cleft in his chin, and had nicked it often in his zeal to achieve the perfect shave.

While he was looking in the mirror after he was done, Larry saw the last several hours flash by as though he were traveling on a rocket: Macon disappearing ahead of him in the darkness.... The dream of being buried by

81

people who didn't know where he was trying to lead them.... Finding his way back.... The travel agent opening a brochure and pointing to a spot on a map....

He bolted out of the bathroom and took the stairs to the attic two at a time.

"I can't believe I didn't see this before!"

"What?" Jessie turned to him, startled.

"What that travel agent was getting at!"

"What?" Jessie asked, confused but now clearly intrigued.

Larry restlessly paced the attic. "See, I didn't have any idea where to go when I walked in there. I just had the idea that with the time off and the kids' spring break, we might as well take a real vacation. And I was confused by all the possibilities. She asked me to look six months into the future and visualize you, me, David, and Jennifer, sitting around looking at photographs of our vacation and reminiscing about all the great things we did together."

"Well, that's a good approach. Of course, it might have been easier for you to visualize that if you'd asked us to help. Then you could be more sure you had a vision all of us shared."

"Yeah, that's just it, Jess. I've been so preoccupied with myself lately, what *I* want and need, that I really didn't see the three of you in the scene. It was just me, looking at this huge, record sailfish I caught. I had only part of the picture." Glumly, Larry admitted, "And now I realize it wasn't the right picture anyway."

"Well, it might be," Jessie said, taking his hand in both of hers. "It's just that you had no way of knowing without including us. And since you didn't consult me, I was offended, and my first impulse was to reject your vision, since you didn't even think to involve me in it."

At once, Larry recalled a voice from his dream. Hadn't it said something to him about going in the wrong direction? What direction was the right one? What was in his future? His team's future? And if he knew the answer to that, worked with his team to *create* that answer, wouldn't it help illuminate the present?

Now he felt an incredible stillness surround him even as his blood raced.

"You know, I just realized that I've gotten in the habit of making all the decisions because I'm the boss, and thinking that because I'm the boss everyone's just going to follow along. And in fact, they have been *trying* to follow, but they didn't know where I was going, didn't see what I saw. So the distance between us has gotten greater, and they've lost heart." He started pacing around the room.

"You're talking about work again," Jessie sighed and frowned, putting down her brush.

"Of course," Larry said, and continued where he'd left off, too excited to notice Jessie's disappointment. "And they don't know where we're going because they didn't participate in shaping the vision. I'm not just talking about building elevator systems and escalators and conveyors. It's the whole thing. How we are going to work together, build the kind of team that can beat our goals, beat our competitors, thrill our customers, create something sustainable, and set ourselves apart from the rest of the pack.

"I've got these guys off in their silo, working on the development of an elevator sub-system, another sub-team in another silo working on a stress-cracking study for the elevated conveyors. What I don't have them doing is talking to each other; teaching, learning from, and challenging each other; and learning to work as one team.

"All I've taught them is to go off and focus on their own pieces of the puzzle and let me worry about putting it all together. I'll bet that some of them, like me, are so focused on the budgets and timelines related to what they're designing and building that they hardly if ever even think about the people who will use it!"

Larry had both hands on his head as he continued, heels of his hands against his temples as though to keep his head where it was. He walked to the window, looked out, then turned around.

"I've been complaining that my team is just dragging along behind me like an anchor, waiting for my lead and then slowing me down. But I really haven't been leading them at all. All I've been doing is watching the daily numbers, pushing, pulling, complaining, and worrying about a future without features, obscured by gloom.

"I've scrutinized all the drawings, blueprints, Gantt charts, PERT charts, budgets, proposals, and contracts. I talked with the customers and designers and suppliers about metal finishes and acceptable noise levels. But I never looked at the kind of team we'd need to become, and I never thought to include all my team members in defining what we'd accomplish, other than meeting the commitments *I'd* made for *them*. All along I've been looking for an answer to what's wrong with my team, but I never asked the right question."

"So what's the question?" Jessie prompted, her voice rising to echo Larry's excitement.

"I think it's this: *Do I have a clear view of the future I am striving to create, and does my team share that same view?* I know it means I'm responsible for knowing where I see us going, but it also means finding a way to involve my team members in helping to shape the vision of the future *we're* going to create. Together."

"How about your family? How about me?" Jessie asked, taking Larry's hand.

"What do you mean?"

"Well, I can't answer for the kids. Jenn may have made plans with her friends, seeing how none of us expected to see much of you this week. And I know David had some glimmer of hope that you'd find the time to take him to a ballgame. But as for me, do you see any pictures of us dancing under a Caribbean moon?"

Larry could share Jessie's romantic image. It even, if only for a second, drove away his image of a big neon sign hanging above the desk in his office, its bright letters spelling: KNOW. When he went downstairs, he opened his laptop and typed in his first important leadership question:

The KNOW question:

Do I have a clear view of the future I am striving to create, and does my team share that same view?

CHAPTER THIRTEEN

"Grow"

The next morning, Saturday, before the Parkses scattered in their various directions, the whole family sat down and talked about Larry's idea for a vacation. Larry and Jessie had agreed the previous evening that he would present his plan as just an idea, not a done deal. If everyone didn't share his enthusiasm, they'd either scrap the idea or make different plans that everyone could be passionate about.

Larry shared his vision of snorkeling, sailing, exploring, dancing, and—oh, yes—fishing. Jennifer said she didn't have any big plans for spring break other than a couple of trips to the mall. David confessed to being disappointed that they weren't going to a ballgame, but Larry promised to get tickets to the doubleheader coming up the weekend after next. And soon everyone had developed some enthusiasm for the trip.

"Great!" said Larry, deeply relieved. "Hey, David, how about you and I go check the Internet for fishing reports and charters?"

"I don't see why *I* don't get to go fishing," Jennifer protested. "How come you always assume it's something only you and David would enjoy?"

Larry hadn't expected that and found himself feeling defensive as he said, "I don't know, I guess, you know, because Mom doesn't enjoy it, I just assumed—"

Then David cut in, "Yeah, Dad. And maybe you don't remember, since you yourself were having so much fun, that the last time we went fishing, in Key West, I spent the whole time barfing over the stern rail and wishing I were dead. I sure can't wait to do *that* again." He turned to Jennifer and, smiling, said, "But, hey, maybe that's something *you'd* enjoy!"

Jennifer wrinkled her face at him and said, "The only thing that makes me nauseous is you."

Then Jessie, recognizing that what often began as playful taunting between their kids might turn ugly if they forgot they were playing, broke in, "All right, all right. So a little fine-tuning is in order. We can work out all the details together, okay?"

Larry smiled in relief, and everyone agreed that the problem was manageable.

"So," Jennifer said, "*I'll* be on the computer."

"That's my girl," Larry said, beaming at his new fishing buddy.

Jessie added, "While you're doing your research, I think I'll go find out where your father and I can take some emergency dance lessons."

"Great idea," Larry said, his voice betraying playful sarcasm. "Meanwhile, David, don't you and I have a ballgame to get ready for this afternoon?"

"You mean you're coming?" David said, incredulous, recalling all the recent Saturdays when his father had apologized with a curt, "Sorry, David, but I have to work." Thinking about a presentation he'd heard just that week at a Future Leaders seminar at school, David wondered if his father knew the difference between what a person *has* to do and what a person *chooses* to do. But he held his tongue—at least today his father was making the right choice.

Larry sat in the stands in the bright sunlight beside Bill, the father of another boy on the team. The two men had become casual friends back when Larry saw more games. They caught up briefly over the first few innings. Then Bill leaned over and said, "David's looking a little distracted out there today. What's up?"

"Nothing I know of," Larry said. He thought about it a little more. "Could be he's thinking about our vacation on Monday. I kind of dropped that on him as a surprise this morning. Or maybe he's worried about the numbers he's been putting up lately: too many strikeouts, couple of fielding errors the last few games. I think he's been trying too hard, putting too much pressure on himself."

"Bull. You can *never* try too hard," Bill insisted. "Look, if he expects a college scholarship, the numbers are everything. Lotta coaches baby their players these days. They're not doing anybody a favor. That business about it's how you play the game, not whether you win or lose—that's a crock. It is *absolutely* whether you win or lose. You don't perform, have a seat on the pine. That's how I see it. Only one team wins the World Series."

Larry let out an ironic little laugh, inaudible to his acquaintance. Bill sounded so much like his mentor—and, more recently for reasons he still couldn't quite grasp, his *tor*mentor—Macon. Then Larry remembered himself telling David almost the same thing.

Larry thought about his son's fondness for baseball. David had been a fan since early childhood, a kid who still had the ticket stubs from his first major-league game thumbtacked to his bedpost. That day, when he had sat with his grandfather along the third-base line watching his heroes play in the sun, was the best day he'd ever spent with a grown-up, he had said. He kept the score-cards for all the games he'd watched, even some on TV, in a binder, organized by year, along with other memorabilia from the games.

"Just like an engineer," Larry had boasted to Jessie more than once when comparing David's binder with his own project binders. And just as Macon had encouraged him to focus relentlessly on the bottom line, keeping the stats on near-term achievements, Larry had encouraged David to see the game more in terms of his personal numbers, less in terms of broader team dynamics and accomplishments.

"You can't control what other people do, David, so just pay attention to business and keep your eye on the ball," he'd urged more than once when David had been upset that someone else's fielding error, or failure to execute a sacrifice, had cost the team the game.

With that focus, Larry realized, it was natural for David to view his own performance on a game-by-game basis and to track his own success more than the team's. In junior high he had worried more about his hitting average than about developing as a well-rounded player, and if the team won but he went hitless, you'd have thought they had lost.

Both David and Larry had been ecstatic when the boy made Central High's junior-varsity team. The school was known throughout the region as one where the campus recruiters spent a lot of sunny afternoons. Its varsity team had been state champions four of the past six years. And a good deal of the credit for that record went, rightly, to the head coach, Joe Matthews, a guy who'd played shortstop all the way up to AAA ball before starting a new career as a history teacher.

Since Matthews had come to Central, even the JV team was doing better. Its coach had nineteen years' tenure, but now he was getting more solid performances from the team. David said that coach was the best he'd ever had, though he was still hoping to make varsity and play under Matthews.

Matthews was known statewide for developing the full potential of his players. There were equally gifted athletes all over the state, but Joe Matthews got more out of his team by year's end. Often, the local sports journalists wrote about how Central's players seemed to play "way over their heads." Once, National Public Radio had come to interview Matthews—the high-school coach who had sent more players to the majors than any other in the country.

This week, the JV coach was out sick with the flu, David told Larry on the way to the field, so Matthews was coaching both teams. That meant he was getting his first good look at the younger players in action. Larry considered what David's play might mean to his chances for varsity. Matthews had to see the kid was trying hard—and that meant a lot to the coach.

In the second inning, David made a nice play in the outfield, catching a runner well off base and doubling him up. Right away, Larry's mood improved.

But then David got a bad jump on a deep fly that he should have caught. Larry knew by the sharp crack of the bat connecting with the ball that it was well-hit, but David's reaction was late. When the ball drew its perfect arc against the blue sky and landed out of the boy's reach, his wild, desperate throw missed the cutoff man, allowing a runner to score when the inning should have been over.

And at the plate, David had grounded into a double play, popped out with a meek foul, and put down a badly executed sacrifice bunt that failed to advance the runner. After the bunt, Larry saw his son hanging his head, almost as though wishing he were somewhere else.

Bill tried to encourage him: "Heads up out there, Davey! Look alive!"

David appeared to frown back at the stands.

Bill seemed offended. "How does he expect to make varsity with that kind of attitude?"

"Give him a break, Bill, it's just a game," Larry heard himself respond. He was realizing what had kept him from ever establishing more than a casual relationship with Bill. "Just one game. He's got some good stats to cushion him. He's got the fall season. And he's got all summer to work on his fundamentals. By the way, he hates being called Davey."

"You're only as good as today's performance, Larry," Bill said.

Larry, remembering Bill's bitter tale of being laid off from his management job at a financial-services company, suspected the man was talking about more than just baseball.

Still, Larry fretted about what Coach Matthews was seeing. When David came back to the bench after the bunt, the coach spoke with him seriously for a minute. Larry frowned, wishing he could hear across the field. *Why couldn't Matthews have been on the bench for any other game?* In the end, Central lost by two runs.

Waiting for David to come up the walkway from the field after the game, Larry prepared his standard man-to-man, "keep your chin up" speech. And so he was momentarily speechless when David came out smiling, head high.

"Hey, Pops, d'ja enjoy the game?"

"I guess," Larry managed through his puzzlement.

They walked to the car. "Guess I've had better games, huh?"

"Try not to be too hard on yourself. There'll be more

games. You know, that pitcher's fastball really was awesome."

"Yeah, he was a big guy, too. Guess I'll be seeing more like him when I play varsity next year."

"That's the spirit," Larry said, placing his hand on his son's shoulder. "Eye on the prize."

Opening the trunk for David to put away his equipment, Larry asked, "By the way, what did Matthews say when he called you over in the eighth?"

David was silent for a moment until they pulled out of the parking lot. Then as they blended into the Saturday-afternoon traffic, he said, "I was expecting him to be all over my case, you know. Going zero for three is bad enough, especially with that feeble bunt. But I figured that run I gave away was going to cost me ten extra laps at least."

"You mean he didn't chew you out?" Larry asked. *How does this guy get good play out of anyone?*

David answered excitedly. "Well, he told me I made mistakes, but said that he guessed I knew that and didn't have to hear it from him. And he's right about that. He asked me a couple of questions about when I missed that long fly ball. How did the ball sound to me coming off the hitter's bat? Where was it in relation to the field when it reached the peak of its arc? Then he told me how to put those things together so that I'd be less likely to misjudge deep flies. Then in the locker room, he had me show him my bunting technique, and then he showed me how *he* does it. It's almost like he's catching the ball with his bat, then just laying it down where he wants it to end up."

David paused for a moment, and Larry sensed he was replaying the brief coaching session in his mind.

When David spoke again, Larry realized that the reason he had paused was to let what he was saying sink into his father's awareness. "You know, Dad, how sometimes when you start correcting me, and then you get upset 'cause I look away and don't seem to be paying attention?"

"Yeah?" Larry said, feeling a little defensive, but masking it so that David would feel comfortable continuing.

"Well, with Coach, I didn't feel that way at all. I couldn't get enough of it."

"So how do you feel now?"

"Hungry," David said.

Larry glanced over. His son had a slight smile. David was ordinarily annoyed when Larry pumped him for information—"the Spanish Inquisition," he sometimes called it—but now he seemed to be enjoying this game of withholding, playing with Larry's impatience to know.

"Come on, David," Larry urged. "Could you give me a little more?"

"Okaaaay, hungry enough for eight tacos and a shake."

"David . . . "

"All right, I'm only kidding." David sighed. "Coach Matthews told me I was a lock for making varsity, so I could stop worrying about that and focus on being a part of a team that could win a state championship. He told me he saw a lot of natural ability and good instincts. I could play a lot better, and he wanted to make sure that I knew it. He asked me to stop by and see him after practice in a couple of weeks to get some pointers on getting the throw off from deep right quicker without giving up accuracy. He also said he wanted to do a general assessment of my fielding skills."

"You okay with that?" Larry wondered if David would feel singled out by the request for a remedial session.

"*Okay*?" David replied, his voice rising. "I'm *better* than okay. It's like, I messed up, but it got me a reward, Dad. Go figure! Hardly anyone on my squad gets to work with Coach Matthews until they make varsity. On some teams, if you play the way I did today, you run laps and then sit out the next game. I get a private session with the best coach in the country. You bet I'm okay with that!"

Watching his son wolf down tacos, Larry reflected on what had just passed. David was looking forward to his session with Matthews. He knew he could improve, and he knew the coach would help him. David and his coach shared a vision. He had someone who could help him grow in his ability to work toward that vision.

And what does the coach get out of this? Larry wondered. Well, he got cooperation. Along with the boy's loyalty and admiration. Beyond that, he would get a better ballplayer who could make a stronger contribution to his team. David would play his heart out for Matthews. But why? And how?

Larry heard a voice from deep in his memory, as if it were calling from down inside a well. It was Jim Enos's calm voice, asking a question at his workshop: "Are your people more valuable than they were a year ago?"

When he'd heard Jim say that, Larry's glib, unspoken response had been, *They better hope so, or else they can find another place to work.* But that wasn't the right answer for a leader. What Larry hadn't considered at the time was how his role was to see that the answer was *Yes.*

He thought about the problem with his young design engineer who hadn't adequately grasped the critical-to-quality concepts for the dimensions on the drawings Fred had complained about. Larry realized now how easy it would have been to sit down with him and explain the concept, show how it applied, and then let the engineer demonstrate his understanding. Instead, he'd found it more expedient to revise the drawings himself. In the bargain, he had resented having to do someone else's job as well as his own, and he had failed to fix the root cause of the problem.

I've been wasting my time putting out fires, Larry reflected, *when I could have been designing a fire-resistant system.*

At that moment, Larry decided that when he got back to work he'd figure out how to *grow* the people on his team, in turn strengthening the team and the company. He wouldn't just worry about what the team had to accomplish. He'd find out where each team member was strong and where each needed to develop, provide them all with feedback and coaching on what he'd observed, encourage them to seek and provide feedback to each other, and give them or get them the help they needed as well as the opportunity to further develop and apply their strengths.

That would divert his time and attention from what he'd been considering to be his job: the daily scorecard. But if he was right, the people he took care of would be taking care of the numbers.

Now Larry knew Coach Matthews's secret: All big-shot major leaguers were once just little-shot high-schoolers whose coaches had the talent and vision to keep them shooting. Matthews, and all the other great coaches, made their players continually more valuable to the team, bringing out their full potential by focusing on their development, being their cheerleader, and turning what some saw only as opportunities for criticism and second-guessing into teaching moments.

As soon as he got home with David, Larry went to his laptop, opened a file he'd titled *KNOW* the night before, and reviewed what he'd typed. First he re-saved the file under the title *KNOW-GROW*. Then he typed his second question:

The GROW question:

Are my team members more valuable to our team, to the company, and to themselves than they were a year ago?

CHAPTER FOURTEEN

"Own"

To reach their island, the Parkses took two jets, a twelve-passenger prop plane (Jennifer nervously observed through clenched teeth that they were practically flying on the wing), and a short boat ride (David had worried about nausea, but he got lucky and felt fine the whole way). They arrived at the inn just in time to watch a sunset justly famed for its brilliant finale. The last flash of the sun—oddly, momentarily green as it hit the horizon—seemed to suspend time for the moment before it slipped into the ocean.

Standing on the veranda, Larry sighed. "If only I could leave that kind of impression when I fade away at the end of a long day!"

"A little ambitious for a weary traveler, aren't you?" Jessie teased.

During a late dinner, Larry encouraged David to come fishing with him and Jennifer. Again the teenager begged off: "I'd rather see the fish through a diving mask."

Jessie opted out, too, saying she'd snorkel with David, and then maybe the two of them would rent bikes and see how much of the island they could explore. "Cool," said David. "How about *motor* bikes?"

"I assume you're talking about scooters?" Jessie said.

"Yeah, they rent them here."

After dinner, Larry asked the hotel's concierge to make reservations for two on a charter fishing boat, and also arranged for the scooter rentals.

Before sunup the next morning, Larry and Jennifer walked down to the pier. There were several fishing boats tied up, and they inched along the dock, peering in the dim light at the names on the sterns.

"Can I help you folks?" asked a cheerful voice.

Larry and Jennifer turned to find a young man in a white T-shirt and shorts, carrying a large Styrofoam chest. "Thanks," Larry said. "We're supposed to get on the *Lady Marmalade.*"

"Dat's our boat!" said the young man, with a quick smile. "Jus' follow me." He set off down the pier.

As Larry followed, happy not to have to ask for any more directions, he reflected on how young the man was. *Too young to own a big boat,* he thought. *Maybe the concierge couldn't get anything better on short notice.* But the man hopped aboard a spotlessly clean thirty-eight-foot charter boat.

A tanned, well-wrinkled man in a captain's hat leaned out of the flying bridge. "Parks? Welcome aboard!" he called. "I see you've met Gustave, our first mate. And that's Patrick, our other first mate. Now let's go get some fish!"

"All right!" said Jennifer.

Larry and Jennifer sat on some cushions in the stern and watched the two mates cast off lines and stow away provisions while the captain slowly steered the boat from the dock. The sun rose as they picked up speed, cutting through the early-morning waves. Soon the sky was brightening, changing the water from gray to brilliant aquamarine, then a deeper, navy blue.

Jennifer watched with fascination as the mates tied leaders for the rods and rigged up a variety of baits. Her eyes widened at the ease with which they coaxed fillets from small fish and trimmed them into uniform triangles, the speed with which they threaded leaders and hooks through whole mackerel, the skill of their fingers tying the most complex knots.

Pointing to the mackerel, Jennifer teased her father, "That bait is as big as most of the fish you catch!" Then, turning more serious, asked, "How did they learn to do all that, Dad?"

"Looks like they've had plenty of practice," Larry said.

Gustave glanced up and smiled, then went back to baiting hooks.

But even more than the mates' skill, what impressed Larry was the care with which they cleaned up afterward: scouring the cutting boards, honing their knives, drying everything before stowing it away. The young men did all these tasks in unison, almost without speaking, seeming to communicate with each other by telepathy.

Of course, he thought, *they probably do these tasks nearly every day. But they can't have that many years of experience—they don't look any older than eighteen or so. And there are all kinds of ways of doing a job. These guys seem to work as though nothing in the world is more important than getting things ready for Jenn and me.*

Soon the boat had reached the fishing grounds, where Larry caught a nice wahoo and a couple of good-size bull dolphin fish. But he was far more thrilled to watch Jennifer. Though she was a thin girl, and at just five feet two weighed less than a hundred pounds, Larry marveled at her strength as she battled a blue marlin for almost an hour, the sweat glistening on her straining arms, her line sizzling as it stripped off her reel.

Patrick hovered by Jennifer's side, coaching her on when to let the fish run and when to lift and take up line. Occasionally, if she looked about ready to give up, he'd give her a pep talk: "Come on, girl, heave dat t'ing. You got da might." And Jennifer would respond with a new surge of energy and determination.

Gustave handed Larry a disposable camera, and he gratefully snapped photos of his daughter in action.

At last the marlin was pulled alongside the boat, as sleek and shiny as a steel sculpture. During this delicate task, the captain and the two crewmen worked together almost effortlessly, exchanging roles and backing each other up in the tight quarters around the stern. When Larry finished off the film in the camera, Gustave brought out another for him and took pictures of father and daughter kneeling alongside the fish. But even without the photos, Larry knew he'd never forget the look of pride on Jennifer's face as she watched over the side of the boat as the two mates released her catch back into the blue water, then crumpled onto a cushion.

On the way back to the harbor, Jennifer slept the sleep of the righteously exhausted. Gustave and Patrick began mopping the deck, stowing away tackle, and cleaning the fish they'd kept. Larry went up to the flying bridge. The captain offered him a seat and a Cuban cigar, and Larry accepted both.

"You've got two great mates back there," Larry said, gesturing over his shoulder. "How do you get your guys to perform like that all day? You must pay them well."

"Are you kidding? I hardly pay them anything. They're kids; they work mostly for tips. Hint, hint." The captain winked at Larry. "I'm just lucky, I guess. They love their work. Nothing they'd rather do, as far as I can tell." He pulled his hat down over his thinning hair, then scratched at his deeply lined cheek.

Larry persisted: "Yeah, I can see they love their work, but it's something else. The way they clean and polish everything, you'd think they owned the boat. In fact, that's what Gustave said when he heard what boat I was trying to find: 'That's *our* boat.' "

"Ha! I should be so lucky. There are times when owning a boat's enough to make you hate the ocean and everything in it."

Despite the captain's evasiveness, Larry felt that he was on to something, like the first tug on one of the lines he'd been dragging for days now. "Come on," he said. "You know what I'm getting at. I've been on boats where the mates sat around chain-smoking, and when you asked one of 'em for help they looked at you like you had some nerve interfering with their leisure cruise."

The captain laughed heartily over the roar of the engines. "Sounds like you've gone out with some of my competitors. But seriously, I know the type. In fact, some of 'em have worked for me—though I use the word 'worked' pretty loosely. With some of those guys, at the end of the day I'd ask myself why I was paying them, since I seemed to be doing just about all the work."

"So why are Patrick and Gustave so different? Did you learn some secret about interviewing prospective mates?"

"Interviewing? You gotta be kidding." The captain laughed again, shaking his head. "Okay, look. I wasn't always so lucky. Most the guys I've hired as mates liked the *idea* of being a mate more than they liked doing the job. And to tell you the truth, I can't blame them. I mean, it's a tough, smelly, exhausting job if you do it well. The hours are lousy, the pay's only sporadically good, and sometimes—more often than I'd care to admit, and please don't take offense—they gotta work all day to help a bunch of pampered tourists who feel entitled to VIP treatment and won't listen to anything you tell 'em about fishing. Guys who blame you when they lose a marlin because they were too cocky and impatient to let it run. Big shots, gonna assert their masculinity through brute force."

"Hope you don't count me in that bunch," Larry said.

"If I did, you wouldn't be sitting up here talking to me," the captain assured him. "Anyway, as I was saying, for a while after I came down here and bought my boat, I used to think I could just buy my labor, too—you know what I mean? I wasn't looking for NASA engineers, just some extra hands. Offer a decent wage, give my orders, then sit back and play captain. They had their jobs, I had mine. Frankly, I think I liked my captain's clothes more than I liked being a captain."

"So what changed you?"

"I got tired of being disappointed in the performance of everyone who crewed for me, and I got honest with myself. I realized that the one constant in all those relationships, other than my disappointment, was *me*. The odds of me getting *nothing* but bad mates by chance was so slight that it must have been *me* making them that way. I could buy their labor, but I needed to start *earning* their commitment."

"How'd you do that?"

"Easier than you'd think, actually, once I admitted that *I* was the problem. Picture me, the great captain, giving up responsibility. That's not easy for a captain to do. But I wanted these guys to act like my partners, so I had to help them understand that even though they didn't own this boat, one day they could have their own. So I started talking to them about *our* boat, not *my* boat. Taught 'em everything they wanted to know—not just about fishing, rigging lines, prepping baits, but about reading charts, navigating, maintaining the engine, using the radio. And these two guys wanted to know *everything*. The more I taught them, the more they wanted to learn."

"How long have they been with you?" Larry asked.

"Couple years. Hired 'em both on the same day. They were the two least experienced guys I ever hired, by the way."

"Why hire inexperienced mates?"

"Well, it just wound up that way. It did occur to me that I'd have an easier time with guys who were too young to have developed habits or attitudes I couldn't abide. But what really sold me on these two kids was the answer to one question: 'Who's the most important person on a charter boat?' "

"What's so hard about that?" Larry said with some surprise. "I just read about sailing mostly, but even I know the captain's boss on any ship."

"Ha!" the captain roared. "That's what I heard from most of the guys I talked to. But the two I hired were the two who said, 'The people you take out fishing.' They knew why I was in business. I figured I could rely on them to help me get the kind of word-of-mouth that would build my business."

"Amazing. Now I understand why Patrick kept calling me 'boss' all day. I gotta tell you, it made me feel good, because I could tell he wasn't just greasing me for a tip."

"You'd be surprised," the captain said with a laugh. "Anyway, I told them that how much they earned with me was in part going to depend on the quality of their work, meeting goals for each trip, and we sat down together and went over what they needed to know and do to meet those goals."

"How'd you figure all this out?" Larry asked—all the while thinking, *Why aren't you heading up a company back in the States?*

"Like I said, necessity," the captain answered. "Just got sick and tired of blaming other people for not meeting my expectations and realized that it was my fault they couldn't. I started making my expectations perfectly clear. I let Gus and Pat know where their authority and responsibility began and ended, gave 'em all the information and training they needed to meet my expectations, and gave 'em a financial stake in their success—I pay 'em extra for taking over more of what I had to do myself at first, and I also match their tips.

"I said to 'em, 'You're a couple of smart, hard-working kids, and you seem mature and responsible. So here's how we're gonna work: I'm gonna tell you and show you what needs to be done, and I'll let you figure out how to organize yourselves to do it. You need help figuring that out, ask me. You don't know how to do something, I'll show you. If you're unclear about what I expect, tell me, and I'll try to make it clear. You discover we need something we don't have, let me know, and if I agree, we'll get it. You find yourself having a problem with me or anyone else you gotta work with on this boat, you let me know about it before it becomes a bigger problem, and we'll work it out together.' That kind of stuff.

"I really knew it was working when one day they came to me at the end of a long, messy trip, and Gustave said to me, 'Captain, we got an idea for the fishing customers.' He and Pat had come up with stocking those little cameras for folks who don't bring their own. I hadn't even had to ask—they were taking the initiative."

Larry nodded. Those cameras were a great idea. Already he felt that they had made the trip twice as valuable to him since he could share the pictures with Jess and David. The boat was nearing its harbor, and he gazed at the sails ahead.

"Mind if I ask another question?" Larry said.

"Shoot."

"Well, I hope this doesn't offend you, and I know it reflects my bias. But what led you down here to run a charter boat, when a guy like you could be back in the States running a big company?"

"No offense taken. Fishing and boating's really what I love. Can you blame me? What more do I need to own?" His outstretched arm swept the expanse of the sea and the aquamarine bowl of the harbor, the gleaming, white-washed government buildings with their fire-engine-red roofs standing out against the green hills.

The captain put down the cigar and stood up to signal his mates that he was throttling back to enter the harbor channel. Then he continued: "But since you mention it, I did spend some time trying to run a company back in the States. Just about ran it into the ground and took a golden parachute." He laughed. "Anyway, I landed down here, bought a boat, and after a while I learned how to be a good captain. I found out that a crew's only as good as its captain. And that if I wanted a great crew I needed to be a great captain."

Larry was almost knocked over by the force of what he

was hearing. He could hear the sound of "OWN" falling into place like a puzzle piece alongside "know" and "grow."

Not so long ago, Larry remembered, Jim Enos had posed a question in his workshop: "Do the people on your team perform like your partners?" The first time he heard that, Larry's thought was, *Who cares, just so long as they do their jobs?* But now he realized it was of central importance, and he began to think about what he could do to begin developing his team's ownership once he got back to work.

Larry added up all the implications of this insight in his head: *If my people know and value where we're going, have the skills and motivations to get there, and believe in their hearts that we're all partners in it together, then we can accomplish great things. And it's my job to establish those conditions. How I do my job is the sum of Know, Grow, and Own.* Larry realized then, at last, what his job was. And how little resemblance it bore to the job he'd been trying to do. He asked the captain for a piece of paper and a pen, and he wrote:

The OWN question:

Do the people on my team perform like hired hands or as if they're partners in business with me?

CHAPTER FIFTEEN

Know-Grow-Own

As much as he had loved his vacation time with his family, Larry was excited to get back to work the next week. Even though—or, actually, especially because—his first task would be a meeting with Chloe.

As they sat down on Monday morning, Chloe said, "So, Larry, I sent you an e-mail about the fabricators while you were away, and I didn't hear back from you. Were you able to respond to that problem?"

"Sure did. I managed to check e-mail a couple of times during the week. I sent that message on to Maria and Phil, with a little guidance. By Sunday they had a plan that I think will save us about a quarter-million dollars—plus two weeks on the lead time for the tooling, to boot. Sorry I didn't close the loop with you about it."

"No problem. That's great!" Chloe said. "Would you mind sharing the details with me?"

"Sure. When Farnum announced Chapter 11 and laid off most of the engineers working with us on those fabricators, I never would've guessed we'd come out in better shape. But Phil and Maria already had a contingency plan they never even told me about. But I'd rather *they* take you through their response, since they know the details of it better than I do."

Chloe's brow furrowed, and Larry couldn't figure out whether that meant concern or confusion. So he asked, "Is something bothering you, Chloe?"

"I was just wondering if you're Larry Parks or someone masquerading as him," Chloe joked.

"Why do you say that?" Larry asked, surprised. But as he spoke, he realized he didn't feel at all like the same man who'd left in a funk just a little over a week ago.

"Come on, Larry, you must be joking," Chloe said, then grimaced. "When was the last time you passed up an opportunity to micro-analyze the numbers? And I'd have expected you to be livid about Maria and Phil having a plan they hadn't told you about."

"Oh, sure, I've spoken with them about that. But I figure there's a reason for their behavior. Either they found me to be unapproachable—and everyone knows I've been pretty grouchy recently—or else they didn't view me as a trustworthy partner. Anyway, it's water over the dam now. I'm determined to change my behavior so that none of the team feels the need to keep things from me." Even as Larry spoke about his old behavior, he felt as if he were describing memories from deep in his past. "But listen, I want to show you what I was working on last night."

Chloe sighed. Larry couldn't help but chuckle at how she must be thinking, *Here it comes—a vast spreadsheet of what-if scenarios.* But he opened his organizer and pulled out a single sheet. Chloe's eyes widened as she read its message:

Leadership Credo
My Team Needs to KNOW
- Do I have a clear view of the future I am striving to create, and does my team share that view?

My Team Needs to GROW
- Are my team members more valuable to each other, to the company, and to themselves today than they were a year ago?

My Team Needs to OWN
- Do the people on my team perform like hired hands or as if they're partners in business with me?

Chloe looked up from the page with a broad smile. Larry noticed her straight, white teeth. The jaw that he'd so often seen as intimidating now seemed merely strong. He wondered if that was because it had been so long since she'd smiled at him like this.

"Larry, I can't tell you how relieved and gratified I am to see this change in you. It seems as though your vacation has done you, and us, a world of good. You just saved yourself and me at least a week, and perhaps a million dollars for the company. Why not go and lead your team? I know they'll be glad to have you back."

"Thanks, Chloe." He got up to leave, and at the door almost ran into Bob Passentino from HR.

"Everything okay?" Bob asked, looking briefly and uncertainly at Larry, then searchingly at Chloe.

"Yes, Bob," Chloe said, and nodded. "Everything is great." She leaned back in her mesh desk chair and smiled. Larry walked briskly down the hall toward his office.

CHAPTER SIXTEEN

Know-Grow-Own Comes Alive

Larry started the team meeting around the conference table in the project "war room" by passing out and explaining his new KNOW-GROW-OWN credo. He answered a few questions about it, then said, "I'm not saying that this is the only way to rejuvenate our project and get it back on track, or even the best way. It's just the way that it occurred to me. I'm sure there are other ways to help people to know, grow, and own, and if any of you has another idea or approach, I'd be glad to hear it after our meeting today.

"Anyway, let's give this a try." Larry leaned toward his team. Maria and Phil, the mechanical engineers, were in a good mood because their contingency plan had worked beautifully. But others, like John, the lead designer, and Eileen, the quality engineer, seemed a bit dispirited. And Fred from manufacturing was his usual gruff self: Larry knew he had the man's respect as an engineer but still had to earn it as a leader.

"First, I want to thank each of you for keeping the project moving forward during my absence, and I want to give you my commitment to providing the kind of leadership from now on that will make you all feel proud and rewarded to be members of this team.

"Our purpose today, as I've already suggested, is to bring the Singapore project back on track and establish a reliable process to keep it there. In doing that, I want us to focus on the positive aspects of what we *can* do, rather than rehashing all our missteps—and we all know we've had enough of that. We're going to reinvent ourselves with a fresh vision of success. How does that sound?"

Larry saw nods of agreement and comments of affirmation. Smiles blossomed before his eyes. "Great." "Excellent." "Let's go for it."

"Great, then let's get started. Imagine that it's two years from today. The Singapore installation went on line two months ago. Everything proceeded according to plan. In fact, we had *even better* outcomes than we could have imagined. Dream with me: What were those great outcomes?"

Fred, generally the first to challenge anything new, spoke: " 'Scuse me, chief, but we have some serious problems with this project, and I don't see how spending a day dreaming about the future is gonna help us solve those."

"Fair enough, Fred, and I really do appreciate the seriousness of our problems. That's exactly why we're here today."

Fred looked quizzically at Larry but let him continue.

"I know this is going to make me sound excessively self-important, but I've had time during my absence to reflect on this project, and many of the common threads I've found in our problems trace back to my leadership—or *lack* of leadership. So, if you'll just indulge me, I believe you'll find this exercise more than worthwhile."

Fred conceded, "You're the boss." He pursed his lips in a way that Larry interpreted as a willingness to be open-minded, which was all he could ask for.

Larry walked to a flip chart, speaking as he went: "Picture that it's two years from now, we've completed our project, and, as I said, we achieved exceptional results. No one thought that we could do it, but we found a way. You all know what our three big areas of concern were."

Around the room people called out, "Speed," "Cost," and "Quality."

"That's right. We were concerned about how fast we could get the job done, how much we could cut the cost to completion, and how well we would delight our customers. I want you to apply your creativity in those three areas. Give free rein to your imagination for a couple of minutes and write down some answers to the question, 'What fantastic results did we achieve?' I'll record your visions."

On each of three flip charts arranged around the room, Larry recorded his team's ideas in the categories of speed, cost, and quality, working with them to reach one solid vision in each area. As he described it, that vision had to be "Good, ambitious, and worthwhile—challenging, but doable."

Under Speed, the team settled on "On line three months early." Fred winced but hung in there.

> ## SPEED
> On Line Three Months Early

Under Cost, they agreed on a big outcome: "Underspent by $2.5 million in manufacturing costs."

> ## COST
> Underspent by $2.5 million

As he turned to another chart and titled it "Quality," Larry realized that with this one he had to remind his team to think beyond technical terms like critical-to-quality parameters. "Put yourselves in the minds of our customers," he told them, "as well as the people who'll use the systems we're building. Think of what we want our customers to say about our work and their relationship to our team."

The team members projected themselves into the future and, from there, started looking back. Maria brought up a statement she'd heard from a customer after a smaller installation had gone live without a hitch: "If I thought I could entice you guys away from KGO, I'd hire this team in a heartbeat." After some discussion, that became the expression of their third dream goal.

> ## QUALITY
> I would hire this team in a heartbeat.

"Okay!" Larry said, almost triumphantly. "Do you see that we've now developed half of our *know* component? We have a clear vision of the future we're trying to create. Now let's answer the question, 'How in the world did we achieve these marvelous results?' We need to add an understanding of the actions and tasks that made those outcomes happen. So here's the first key question: What do you believe you *did* to enable us to bring in the project three months early?"

Larry turned to the flip chart titled "Speed" and collected the input his team volunteered.

SPEED ("KNOW")

On Line Two Months Early

1. Negotiated with customer to reduce testing cycle by 25% without jeopardizing safety, quality, or product integrity.
2. Employed "extreme programming" technique to reduce programming time by 20%.
3. We addressed our unresolved interpersonal conflict.
4. Increased by 30% the number of tasks done concurrently rather than in straight-line sequence.
5. Reassigned underused technicians on site back to support project work at the home office.

"Powerful stuff!" Larry said, shaking his head in admiration as they examined their list. The ideas for speed also promised good results for cost and quality, and these showed up as the group generated *know* sheets for the other two areas.

When the team had completed the *know* part of the exercise, Larry said, "Now let's turn to *grow*. And the key question here is, 'Looking back at what we accomplished, and how we accomplished it, what new education, skills, and capabilities did we acquire that made it all happen?' "

As his team shouted out their ideas, Larry walked to the *grow* sheets he had taped on the front wall for speed, cost, and quality and listed them. Being engineers, the team offered mostly highly technical "what" skills at first, but soon, with Larry's coaching, they got to some critical "how" issues. The cost sheet, this one, contained some great ideas.

COST ("GROW")

Underspent by $2.5 million

1. Lead engineers received advanced training in Quality for Design.
2. Brought in university consultant to help reliability engineer with latest ideas in tolerance analysis.
3. Scheduler taught team the newest developments in Critical Project Milestones.
4. All meeting leaders trained in group facilitation.

---

5. All supervisors trained in coaching and mentoring.

6. Outside consultant brought in to do team-building exercises and help us resolve our conflicts.

The spirited discussion of the *grow* ideas made it clear to everyone that the team had plenty of room for development. Eileen observed that if they actually learned those skills, not only would that benefit the Singapore project, but they'd be bringing powerful new capabilities to other parts of KGO as well. "We can accomplish *anything*," she said.

Several people chorused, "Amen."

But Larry noticed one member looking at the chart and frowning. "Sam?" he coaxed. "Do you have a concern?"

Sam shrugged, slouched a little in his seat, then said, "It's just with the last few items. This seems like going back to all that soft flavor-of-the-month training, and I still don't see their relationship to cost." He sat back with his arms folded over his chest.

Larry nodded and offered, "I hear you, Sam. And it wouldn't surprise me if others of you actually feel the same way, because I was right there not too long ago." He scanned the room and saw another team member look down when he met his eyes.

Then he continued. "Here's what I propose. If it's okay with everyone, I'd like to take up your reservations about the soft skills at another time, when I can sit down with you and we can find a way to quantify the cost and value of those items. That'll let us use our time today to forge ahead with our agenda. I'm sure we'll continue to refine it after today. How does that sound?"

Larry recorded Sam's point on an Issues chart, and quickly turned back to him.

"Works for me," Sam said, straightening in his chair and picking up his pen.

"Great, then let's schedule that meeting before we break today, and get back to our cooking." Larry said. "Now, let's get to the payoff. So here's the challenge—and remember, we're still in the future, looking back: 'How did you come to have the feeling of *ownership* that yielded these great results?'

"Or to put it another way, let's imagine our customer, right after pulling the switch, saying, 'If I thought I could entice this project team away from KGO, I would hire it in a heartbeat!' Given some of the glitches that were occurring two years before, what has caused the customer to see that level of commitment in you?

"To get at this, I think we should divide the actions into three groups. First, what kind of behavior on *your* part demonstrated that ownership? Second, what did *I* do as your leader to make you feel more like partners than like hired hands? And third, what role did KGO, and Excalibur in particular, play in encouraging your feelings of partnership?"

The team's ideas on all three questions gushed like water from a spring, and while all three charts for *own* looked really good, the ideas listed under quality were particularly impressive.

QUALITY ("OWN")
I would hire this team in a heartbeat.

We did this:
1. Reduced whining through $1 griping fines.
2. Brought customer to the main office to see our domestic operation, firsthand.
3. Saw the customer as someone to delight rather than someone to satisfy.

Larry did this:
1. Led this KNOW-GROW-OWN exercise two years ago.
2. Delegated more responsibility and authority to us.
3. Showed more interest in our ideas; initiated an idea-of-the-month program.
4. Showed more appreciation for our personal sacrifices and hard work.
5. Openly and honestly addressed conflicts with dignity and respect.

KGO did this:
1. The CEO visited the project team quarterly to show his interest and support.
2. The bonus suggestion plan was reinstated.

"Well, I'm nearly done with the first of the five suggestions you have for me on the quality chart," Larry remarked. "As for the other four, those define the kind of leadership mandate I'm looking forward to fulfilling."

He thought to himself, *I wouldn't have imagined I'd feel so good about taking suggestions at all. And if I'm surprised about how I'm reacting, imagine how the rest of the team feels!* But they didn't seem skeptical; they seemed genuinely pleased with what they were seeing.

By then, it was five o'clock. Larry had to tell his team that it was time to stop. Phil protested that they didn't want to leave—there was still work to be done. But Larry responded, "Folks, I have a family expecting me for dinner. And so do some of you. But listen, first thing tomorrow morning, we're going to come back and start turning our vision into reality.

"The first step will be to weed out duplication among our ideas on these nine charts. Then we'll prioritize all those that remain. According to Pareto's Law, we'll need to implement only twenty percent of the best ideas to achieve eighty percent of our three visions. And that will have us all on cloud nine in two years. So tomorrow morning, I'll bring the bagels and donuts."

The team applauded, and when Fred stood and saluted him, crisply yet playfully, Larry almost got choked up.

CHAPTER SEVENTEEN

Out of the Woods

Larry Parks didn't get to see the end of the Singapore project as team leader. Four months before the installation was to go on line, Chloe Hall was promoted to Executive Vice President for Sales, based in Europe. And out of all her managers, she recommended that Larry succeed her as Vice President for Engineering. He was still getting used to his new corner office with a view of the woods on the day the Singapore project was complete.

Larry sent an invitation to Fred, who'd taken over leadership of the project, to bring the project team into his office at the start of the day and read the e-mail messages from the construction managers and their customer reporting complete success. The team applauded and toasted the project with orange juice and muffins. "Speech!" Fred called out, with a wink since he knew Larry wasn't a comfortable public speaker.

But Larry did want to say something to his old team. He cleared his throat, and the group quieted. "Thanks, everyone. This project has been a major part of my professional life, even more than you may know.

"About two and a half years ago, I was given the chance to manage a project with goals I considered unreachable and a team I convinced myself was mostly unmanageable. I spent the next six months proving myself right. We missed one milestone after another, and one employee after another, suffering under my lack of trust and my poor leadership, threatened to leave the team. A couple of them actually did.

"But then, I went away for a little while and stumbled into a new way of thinking about my job. You all know the basics."

"Know, grow, and own!" the team chorused, amid chuckles.

"That's right." Larry grinned. "When I came back, we were behind our schedule, over our budget, and barely communicating with each other. But we set ourselves three very ambitious goals. Do you remember these?" He pulled the old flip-chart pages out of his desk drawer, the paper wrinkled and yellowing but the words clear.

The team murmured in surprise at the sight of those old pages. "Larry, we gotta get you a recycling basket," Eileen joked.

Larry smiled back but continued: "I want to look at how well we did on those goals. Back then, we were on the cusp of notifying our customer that we projected a delay of six weeks. Then we set a goal of finishing three months early. And the optimism we generated that day encouraged us to hold off on formally notifying Singapore of the delay. And it was a good thing we did. We made up the six weeks we thought we'd lost and picked up another four. We finished a month ahead of schedule!"

The team cheered and raised a toast.

"As for cost," Larry continued, "we suggested two-point-five million in savings. That never was realistic. We came in *only* eight hundred and fifty thousand under budget. I emphasize 'only' because—I looked this up—you'd have to go back eleven projects and four years at Excalibur to find one that managed to save that much money."

More cheers.

"Finally, there was our great expectation for quality. Now, our customer didn't fulfill our fantasy of recruiting the project team at twice our regular salaries—"

"Awwwww," chorused Larry's audience, clearly enjoying the strong team spirit they had developed. That wouldn't keep them from accepting twice the pay from another company, Larry knew, but they probably weren't sending out their résumés. Employee departures were low, and even Dave had asked to return to the same team after his "sabbatical."

"Our customer didn't recruit us," Larry added, "but it did give this team several glowing endorsements to other companies in Asia, and last week Chloe turned those into the largest contract in KGO's history!"

Three months later, Chloe asked Larry to come over to London for a month to teach a new project-leadership course. After speaking to his family, he agreed. "I think you really have something to say," Jess said. "Plus, David will be at training camp that month, and it would be good for Jennifer to see Europe—not to mention good for me."

On the first day of the course, Larry looked into the audience, fighting a mild case of stage fright. The twenty people gathered were many of Excalibur's top engineers, both new hires and tenured high-potentials. Some of them were on their first leadership assignments, and others were being groomed for new important projects. Chloe introduced Larry warmly as "one of KGO's great success stories" and turned the stage over to him.

"Folks, I'm not a public speaker," he started. "And I'm not a trainer. All I ever wanted to be was an engineer, which is what I do best. Along the way, someone—" He eyed Chloe and smiled. "Someone with vision believed enough in me to think I could also become a leader. And through a combination of luck and necessity, maybe I did.

"For any of you who wonder how I managed that, I'll be happy to share the details of my journey later. But the most important part was that I figured out that *how I led* meant everything to what my team could achieve.

"When I tell you what I learned, I expect many of you will shake your heads in disbelief that it took me so long to wise up. You'll ask what the big deal is about the simple leadership message you're about to hear. You'll think, 'Isn't what he's saying just common sense?'

"Well, I'm standing here as proof that common sense isn't so common. Many people never get the message I'm about to share with you. Many of the ones that have it figured out still can't convert what they know in their heads into action. And maybe a big reason for that is that they're not honest with themselves *about* themselves.

"I'm a great example of this. At first, I thought I could get my boss off my case just by filling my head with the right terms and spouting platitudes. So I agreed to go to leadership training. I pleased myself with my ability to make it sound like I was ready to 'empower my team.' I even fooled myself into thinking that I really had learned how to get better results.

"But it wasn't until I got the learning into my *heart*—it wasn't until I dropped my defenses and took off my mask—that I was able to open myself to the need for change. And I had to make a one hundred-eighty-degree turn to keep myself from heading further down the wrong road. There are many ways to find the right road. My journey is just one of them. But today, we're here to make sure you set off in the right direction from the start."

Larry then asked all the participants to introduce themselves and their work. They came from all parts of KGO's operations, and many engineering specialties.

Nodding, Larry resumed: "What a great combination of experience and talent we've got in this room! As I said before, what we're about to cover isn't rocket science. It's not even escalator science. In fact, the very heart of this course—the *know-grow-own* trinity—is easy enough for a twelve-year-old to grasp. But it may also be *easier* for a twelve-year-old to *apply* than for some of the people in this room.

"If you're anywhere near where I was when I first heard

about these three leadership mandates, you'll have two reactions. You'll either believe you're already fulfilling them, or you'll think they sound like a prescription for hand-holding. To put it differently, if you're like the Larry Parks I once knew, *you just don't get it.*

"I hope you're not where I was two and a half years ago. But just in case you are, I want to share with you a list of some of the reasons why managers—just like me back then—don't get it. And if you want to know where this list came from, it's partly my autobiography, and it's partly inspired by a few other Larry Parkses I've met."

Larry turned to a flip-chart page that he had prepared that morning:

Why Managers Don't Get It
They focus on platitudes
They're in denial
They resist change
They make excuses
They believe output always trumps process
They're arrogant
They think "soft side" is for "soft minds"
They think leadership is magical

"During today's session, we'll be filling in the blanks on this list with examples of what you've heard other people say and seen them do that demonstrate these attitudes. Then I'll ask each of you to identify where you might be in this list. And I'll lead that discussion by showing you how many items on that list applied to me."

By the end of the day, as Larry promised, the list had been fleshed out:

Why Managers Don't Get It

They focus on platitudes
- not walking the talk
- faking it through the day

They're in denial
- "That's not really me"
- "But I'm doing my job"

They resist change
- "This fad will pass"
- "No one complained before"

They make excuses
- "It's not my fault"
- "In my last company we didn't do it this way"
- "I've had a run of bad luck"

They believe profit always trumps process
- "Don't tell me *how* to do my job, just tell me *what* needs to be done"

They're arrogant
- "I don't need other people to tell me whether I'm doing a good job"
- "I'm the boss; I've made it by being who I am"

They think "soft side" is for "soft minds"
- "People need to be watched"
- "Nice guys finish last"

They think leadership is magical
- "Leaders are born, not made"
- "You've either got it or you haven't"

In the discussion that followed, Larry was gratified to hear about how participants would be able to apply these insights to developing themselves and others. All but three participants owned up to being guilty of at least one of the barriers on the *don't-get-it* list. "A good start, people," he said at the end of the day. "I'm looking forward to seeing you tomorrow, when we'll talk about the specifics of assembling a project team."

Most of the participants filed out, talking about their respective projects or restaurants they wanted to try in that part of London. But one young engineer stayed behind, approaching Larry tentatively. "My name's Joel," he said, forgetting the nametag stuck to his shirt. "I know this training is really going to help me get my project off to a good start."

"That's good to hear," said Larry. *But what's worrying you?* he thought.

And indeed, Joel was struggling to say something more. Larry smiled, assumed an open posture, and waited.

"It's just that I still feel much more comfortable with the 'hard side,' the numbers," Joel said.

"Good. I still value the numbers, too," Larry assured him. "Doing that makes you a good engineer *and* a good manager. But it's not all there is, and often in focusing on the numbers we don't see all of them or what they mean. Besides, the key is that you need to develop other qualities, too, to become a good *leader.*"

"But how? What's the way to *get it*?"

"There isn't any *one* way to get it," Larry replied. "I found lessons in my life from visiting a travel agent, watching my son play baseball, fishing with my daughter, and listening to my wife. But I bet I could have found them in other ways as well, had I been open to them."

Larry snapped his briefcase shut. Joel still seemed puzzled. "Have you got an hour for coffee?" Larry asked him. "They have coffee in London, right? If you want, I can tell you the whole story about how *I* got it. I had to learn my lessons the hard way. I was the type who had to nearly hit rock-bottom before I realized which way was up."

As they sat in the dark coffee shop on their second refill, listening to the music of Louis Armstrong, the younger man said, "Thanks for taking the time—that's quite a story. I have to admit, though, that what you're telling me about 'rock-bottom' sounds pretty scary."

"Yes, but this story has a happy ending, right?"

"Yes it does," Joel said, then added, "You know, for a guy who claims not to be much of a speaker, you tell a heck of a good story. Ever think about writing all this down in a book?"

"Now *there's* an idea," Larry chuckled, entertained by the thought of himself as a writer.

"Any idea what you'd call it?"

"I'm not sure about that, Joel. But I think I know how it ends."

"How's that?"

"I made it out of the woods: I was lost, and now I'm found."

From the Authors

We wrote *Lost & Found* in response to one of the most common challenges we encounter in our consulting and coaching assignments: A new (or not-so-new) manager whose record of technical competence has earned him a promotion to a position of leadership but who's failing because that responsibility requires a new set of interpersonal and motivational skills for working with people.

In our approximately seventy-five years of collective experience as consultants and coaches, we've met thousands of Larry Parkses. Their technical competence has led to accolades and promotions. But they lack a comparable level of people skills, perhaps because they view them as "soft," too "touchy-feely," and inherently ambiguous. And the leadership training workshops to which they've been sent—either for preparation or remediation—haven't done the trick: They learn to talk the talk, but they don't really absorb the essence of leadership, and they return to their jobs much as they left: competent at the work but deficient as leaders.

Our hero, Larry, learned to *walk* the talk by discovering the KNOW-GROW-OWN lessons captured in his Leadership Credo. Our experience convinces us that this credo will help managers in all kinds of organizations: large and small, privately held and publicly traded, manufacturing and service, private-sector and public-sector, operating within a single zip code and operating transnationally. The three tenets of Larry's credo reflect fundamentals in human behavior—truths not bound by the specific organization in which leaders execute the credo.

We hope that this book has helped you "out of the woods," and that you believe in the power and potential of fulfilling your team members' needs to KNOW, GROW, and OWN. But we realize that you may still wonder about how to actually put those ideas to work and develop flexible strategies and techniques to harness their power and potential in your own company. In Larry's story we provided one example: a team retreat built on retrospective visioning. Larry asked his team members to imagine an ideal future, work together to define it, and then outline the tactics required to produce that state. Larry facilitated the discussion so that the tactics fulfilled the KNOW-GROW-OWN needs.

But Larry also stated, "I'm not saying that this is the only way to rejuvenate our project and get it back on track, or even the best way. It's just the way that it occurred to me. I'm sure there are other ways to help people to know, grow, and own. . . . " We all know there indeed are other ways, and one may fit your situation better than another. For you, it's important to be able to draw from a reservoir of strategies and tactics.

On the following pages we offer some tips for finding and implementing strategies that fulfill your organization's KNOW-GROW-OWN needs. We aim to describe the range of possibilities rather than to catalog them (which would require another book, at least). We provide examples of approaches that, in our experience, are most likely to bring maximum benefits to the greatest number of leaders and organizations. But we also hope that considering the tips and principles behind them will inspire you and your teams to generate alternatives tailored for your particular needs.

We present these tips in three sections: *Tips to KNOW, Tips to GROW,* and *Tips to OWN*. Each section starts with a defining question.

Even though KNOW, GROW, and OWN are three distinct leadership requirements, a strategy may fulfill two or three simultaneously—in fact, in today's pressured organizations, the value of a strategy may lie in how it fulfills more than a single requirement. For example, Larry's retrospective visioning exercise served all three.

Finally, we authors welcome suggestions and success stories from our readers about strategies that you've found useful in realizing the power of KNOW, GROW, and OWN.

Tips to KNOW

Defining Question:
Do I have a clear picture of the future I am striving to create, and does my team share that same view?

Ask "What Can We Become?" Sometimes we get caught up in solving problems that are relics of an irrelevant past. Your team's energy and creativity might be better invested in seeing what *could be* rather than what *is* or *was*. Set aside a significant block of time (1–2 days) and develop both a scenario of the future and plans for making that scenario a reality. Never assume that simply because *you* have a vision for the future your team shares it. Discuss, debate, define, and validate a common perception.

Look Outside Your Office. What are your organization's opportunities and threats? What are your internal strengths and weaknesses? How will you differentiate yourself from your competitors?

Think Strategically, Not Just Tactically. Leaders must do more than focus on short-term goals and operational issues, even though they usually become leaders by succeeding at just those challenges. Get your team involved in making and implementing those tactical decisions so you can concentrate on the bigger strategic picture.

Probe Every Premise. Scrutinize the assumptions under which you and your organization work. Reexamining them might open up new pathways, or reinforce your priorities. Ask, "Is there a better way?"

Convene Open Forums. Seek opportunities to answer questions from your team about the organization, where it is, where it's going, and any issues that affect its goals. The best forums are conducted face to face, but you can keep them going through electronic chat rooms or newsletters. Assure all participants that they can probe issues without fear of recrimination. Make your answers as candid and accurate as possible.

Share the Numbers. If you're being judged on the basis of certain numbers, do the people on your team know those numbers? Do they know why those measures were chosen, and what they translate to? Can they see the progress toward the team goals as well as their particular contributions?

Put Out a Question Box. Ask team members to submit any questions they have about why the company does things in a certain way. Find out the answers, talking to other departments if you need to, and share them with your people. View questions as an opportunity to learn and share.

Get on the Same Page with Your Boss. Write down the ten things you do that you believe make the greatest contribution to your success, with the relative value that you place on them. Schedule a meeting with your boss to discuss how your vision matches his or hers. Make the necessary adjustments before you share your vision with your team.

Create a Vision with Your People. Convene a meeting and tell your team what transformations you're looking for in bottom-line performance (results). Draft these as "from/to's" expressed with their most essential quantitative and qualitative measures—for example, sales rising from "x" this year to "y" in two years; from despair to hope.

Turn Your Vision into Goals. After you establish the "results" you want, ask your team to decide what transformations they need to achieve in these six areas: Clients, People, Sales and Marketing, Operations, Culture, and Strategy. Once they've brainstormed these transformations (as "from/to's") and settled on the three to six most vital transformations from the larger list, your team has a vision for the near term. These strategic priorities should keep everyone moving in the same direction.

Express Your Core Values. Most successful organizations base their efforts on a set of core values, such as Continuous Improvement, Cost Consciousness, or Technical Excellence. Their leaders don't just champion these guiding values, but embed them into employee recruitment, orientation, training, performance evaluation, and day-to-day management. Using surveys, focus groups, and interviews, you can determine the core values guiding your organization, as well as the behaviors that show those values.

Tips to GROW

Defining Question:
Are my team members more valuable to each other, to the company, and to themselves today than they were a year ago?

Growing on the Job Is Part of the Job. Development is an intrinsic part of people's work, not an extra. Training is a benefit, not a burden. Employees should seek training, and bosses should take the responsibility to ensure it happens. Make it practical and timely by linking all training and development to clearly defined business needs.

Make Friends with Your Company's Trainers. Technical training is a must, but technical skills aren't enough for either leaders or employees. Work with your in-house trainers and outside vendors to ensure that your team members can gain the people skills that increase their value to themselves, to you and the team, and to the organization.

Stop Making Yourself and Others Indispensable. Imagine that you're on vacation in the Caribbean, and for a week a hurricane prevents you from flying back or phoning in. Will your team be able to carry on? Identify the crucial knowledge that only you have, and share that with others. Then do the same exercise for all your team members. Would the temporary loss of any one person make the whole team grind to a halt? (Is that what's keeping you from scheduling yourself or others for training?)

Delegate Thoughtfully. When you delegate, think not only about what you need to get accomplished, but about what sort of challenge your employee needs and is ready for. When your needs as a leader intersect with the needs and motivation of that person, you have a great opportunity. Remember: Delegation is neither dumping nor abdication.

Set the Tone Every Day. You may think you can't change the corporate culture, but you're actually helping to build it with everything you do and every word you utter. Your people look to you as a model. So pay attention to the signals you send about what you value and believe in.

Balance Your Training, and Train for Balance. Your training, and the training you arrange for your team members, should cover both people skills and technical skills. Don't feel that you have to choose between them. Leaders, managers, and future managers need *both.* Behind many technical skills is an interpersonal behavior that enables people to perform. Be sure your appraisals cover goals in both areas as well.

Evaluate Your Performance Evaluations. Does giving appraisals make you uncomfortable, leading you to fall back on "the numbers"? Consider asking for training in how to provide non-threatening, constructive feedback. Seeking that skill is a sign of a good leader. (In fact, the part of your job that makes you most uncomfortable is always a clue about what kind of training to seek.)

Turn Performance Appraisals into Coaching Sessions. Regardless of how your organization assesses employees, performance appraisals aren't just about reaching agreement with people on how well they've performed. To be most effective, they also have to include coaching on how to perform better—how to "raise the bar." Do you spend most of your time on how employees can GROW?

Create a "Learning Rich" Working Environment. Employees should feel that coming to work provides an opportunity to enhance their skills and knowledge. They should feel like they have a chance to expand their brain cells, not bury them. Hire smart people to begin with, but create an environment where they can become smarter.

Make sure all your people know about your company's support for continuing education.

Start a Department Library. Provide subscriptions to industry journals, plus general business and news magazines. Add management books, cassettes, and videos for people to take home.

Form a "Brown-Bag Book Club." Once a week, invite employees to eat together and chat about what they've read recently. You could discuss a book on leadership or on innovations in a field related to your business, a news article, notes from a training session or a business seminar. Look at the covers of that week's news magazines, and brainstorm how an event or trend might affect how you do your jobs.

Tips to OWN

Defining Question:
Do the people on my team perform like hired hands or as if they're partners in business with me?

Lead Your Team into Tactical Planning. Issues such as production scheduling, budgeting, purchasing, inventory management, and logistics are appropriate for tactical planning discussions. Convene teams that stretch across organizational boundaries to debate the most effective alternatives. There are no perfect plans, but cohesive teams with a common vision will compensate and ensure that imperfect plans achieve the desired goals.

Resist Finding Solutions Yourself. Rather than solving problems yourself, engage your team in finding solutions.

Offer them tools and tips on how to look for and choose solutions, *facilitate* the finding of solutions, and then help to obtain resources to execute the solution, but make sure that the solution comes from your people.

Ask for Suggestions and Adopt Them. Employees start owning processes and products when they're personally involved in improving them. Ask your team to suggest ways to make your results *better, faster,* and *cheaper.* Form a committee to assess the suggestions and reward employees for them.

Let Others Set Their Own Goals. When people own their work, they take more initiative. People tend to own their work in proportion to the amount of input they have into its content and outcomes. In appraisals and training, encourage your people to take the lead in setting their own goals for the future, and give them feedback on their progress.

Mix Monetary and Non-Monetary Rewards. To inspire people to work *with* you and not *for* you, find ways to feed both the pocketbook and the soul. Charter a team to explore options for creating and dispersing rewards. Check with leaders in your industry and find the best models. Tweak them to fit your organization.

Publicly Recognize People's Accomplishments. When you make recognition public—whether through rewards or simple acknowledgment—you not only show that you care, but you demonstrate a model for the rest of the organization about the kind of performance that stands out. Others will aspire to that level of performance.

Help Employees to Satisfy Their Customers. Regardless of

their job descriptions, all employees must satisfy customers—internal or external. Decrease the distance (physical and psychological) between your team and their customers through team-building activities and cross-functional project teams. Decrease your employees' distance from external customers by sharing their feedback, inviting them to tour your facility, and sharing sales and customer satisfaction data with all employees.

Take a Colleague to Lunch. When important external customers come to town, you probably take them to lunch. How about taking an important internal customer to lunch the same way? And be sure to bring some of your team along.

Show Off a Little. Post letters and e-mails from customers on a team bulletin board, along with articles about the firm. Decorate the walls with photos of your company's products or services being used. Install a "trophy case" to display mementos or product samples from your customers or clients. Post a map with locations of all your projects. Look for a way for your team to "sign" their work.

Look for Things to Brag About. Ask your employees to imagine explaining their work to their kids or their parents. What are they proud of doing? What team accomplishments would make them go home and brag? In what way have your proudest accomplishments made a positive difference for others?

Periodically we all find ourselves "lost in the woods" like Larry Parks. Ruminating about how we got there, finding scapegoats, or berating ourselves for stupid choices will simply keep us in those woods. At some point we must follow Larry's example and find our way out. We hope the ideas we've highlighted will help.

Good luck on your journey.

Lyle Sussman, Sam Deep, and Alex Stiber

ACKNOWLEDGMENTS

Lyle wants to give thanks to my wife, Susan, for teaching me the essence of Know, Grow, and Own; to my children, Sandy and Annie, for teaching me the value of listening; and to the innumerable students and clients I've had over the years for holding me accountable for saying things worth the listening.

Sam is thankful for the strength and support of his wife, Dianne, who in good times and in bad is there to sustain his work and tolerate that his attention is sometimes on "Chapter 7" when it should be on her. This book would have been impossible to conceive without the students and corporate clients who continue to teach leadership to me through their questions, through their setbacks, and through their triumphs. It was in the Carnegie Mellon University freshman English class of Granville "Pete" Jones where I first became inspired to write. Thanks, Pete.

Alex is indebted to the many people who helped him directly and indirectly with this book. In particular, I would like to celebrate my wife, Jill, who never hesitated to tell me exactly what she thought of the book as it developed. To friends who were early readers of the book—especially Don Coop, Mike Mangan, Earl Liebich, Allan McGuffey, and Alistair McHarg—thanks for your encouragement. And to colleagues, mentors, clients, and teachers—in particular, Bill Kline, Susan Kratch, Ben Lane, T. Ballard Morton, Sena Jeter Naslund, and Charlie Wells—gratitude for providing so many opportunities for learning and growth.

We three also wish to express our admiration for our partners at Crown—especially Annik La Farge, our senior editor, who strengthened *Lost & Found* with every perceptive comment she made and with every incisive question she asked.

Finally, to our agent, John Bell, whose ownership throughout the entire process of bringing this book to our readers puts him in a class by himself. He was there when the book was merely an idea, he was there when the idea had become a fully formed book, and he did everything but write dialogue in between. We would not have wanted to try to do what we did without him.

ABOUT THE AUTHORS

Lyle Sussman, Ph.D., is chairman and professor of management at the University of Louisville in Louisville, Kentucky. He is also a former newspaper columnist and acclaimed speaker, executive coach, and seminar leader. His engagements have taken him throughout most of the U.S., Canada, Mexico, Europe, and the Far East. Lyle's clients include the Fortune 500, religious organizations, and trade associations. He has written more than sixty scholarly papers and authored or coauthored eleven books that have been translated into fourteen languages, with approximately a million copies in print worldwide. To learn how you and your colleagues can unleash the power of "Know, Grow, Own," visit Lyle on the worldwide web at www.LyleSussman.com.

Sam Deep helps organizations of all types turn themselves around through leadership development, team building, and strategic action planning. As an adjunct professor of management and strategy, he teaches "Meeting the Challenges of Corporate Leadership" to second-year MBA students at Carnegie Mellon University. Sam's radio show "Lead the Way" on KQV in Pittsburgh is one of few programs in the country directed at improving corporate, government, and educational leadership. His fourteen books have sold more than one million copies in fourteen languages. Sam's half-day "Lost and Found" workshop reveals dozens of practical and proven "Know, Grow, Own" tactics and strategies. To help the managers in your organization become stronger leaders, visit Sam at www.samdeep.com.

Alex Stiber is an organization development professional, as well as a creative writer and author with work published in more than thirty journals and magazines over three decades. In his consulting practice, he has helped clients improve their business results by aligning their cultures, developing their work force, and strengthening the technical and people skills of their leadership. Alex teaches leadership at Duquesne University and has presented on teams and culture at Maynard Forum, Carnegie Mellon University, and elsewhere. His workshop based on the principles in *Lost and Found* helps leaders build on their experience and implement action plans to produce better results by meeting employees's needs for vision, development, and ownership. Visit Alex at www.alexstiber.com.

Here's how to contact the authors of *Lost and Found*:

Lyle Sussman 502-452-1249 lylesussman@louisville.edu

Sam Deep 800-526-5869 sam@samdeep.com

Alex Stiber 412-278-1301 astiber@adelphia.net